Pr

Dor

MW01688639

1992

Hayit Publishing

CARIBBEAN
N
0
500 km
USA
Miami
BAHAMAS
Havanna
CUBA
MEXICO
GREATER
DOMINICAN
REPUBLIC
HAITI
San Juan
JAMAICA
Port
-au-Prince
Santo
Domingo
PUERTO
RICO
CARIBBEAN
Kingston
ANTILLES
SEA

DOMINICAN REPUBLIC
HAITI
Punta Rucia
La Isabela
Playa Dorada
Luperon
Sosúa
Cabarete
Monte Cristi
Puerto Plata
Santiago
de los Caballeros
Río San Juan
Las Terrenas
El Portillo
Las Galeras
Moca
Nagua
Samaná
La Vega
San Francisco
de Macoris
Sánchez
Pico Duarte
Jarabacoa
Los Haitíses
Constanza
Bonao
San Juan
Higüey
La Caleta
Boca Chica
San Pedro
de Macoris
Altos de
Chavón
Punta
Cana
PORT-AU-PRINCE
Lago Enriquillo
Azua
San
Cristóbal
Bani
SANTO
DOMINGO
Juan Dolio
La Romana
Cabral
Barahona
CARIBBEAN SEA
N
0
100 km

<1st> Edition 1992

UK Edition: ISBN 1 874251 10 X
US Edition: ISBN 1 56634 005 5

Author: Peter Hinze
Translation, Adaption, Revision: Scott Reznik
Print: Druckhaus Rombach, Freiburg/Germany
Photography: Peter Hinze, Fr. Scheuba
Distribution to the trade:
UK: Amalgamated Book Service/Kent
USA: National Book Network/Lanham, MD

Printed in Germany

Using this Book

Books in the series *Practical Travel A to Z* offer a wealth of practical information. You will find the most important tips for your travels conveniently arranged in alphabetical order. Cross-references aid in orientation so that even entries which are not covered in depth, for instance ''Holiday Apartments,“ lead you to the appropriate entry, in this case ''Accommodation.“ Thematically altered entries are also cross-referenced. For example, under the heading ''Medication,“ there appear the following references: ''Medical Care,“ ''Travel Medications,“ ''Pharmacies,“ ''Vaccinations.“
With travel guides from the series *Practical Travel A to Z* the information is already available before you depart on your trip. Thus, you are already familiar with necessary travel documents and maps, even customs regulations. Travel within the country is made easier through comprehensive presentation of public transportation and car rentals in addition to the practical tips ranging from medical assistance to newspapers available in the country. The descriptions of cities are arranged alphabetically as well and include the most important facts about the particular city, its history and a summary of significant sights. In addition, these entries include a wealth of practical tips — from shopping, restaurants and accommodation to important local addresses. Background information does not come up short either. You will find interesting information about the people and their culture as well as the regional geography, history and the current political and economic situation.
As a particular service to our readers, *Practical Travel A to Z* includes prices in hard currencies so that they might gain a more accurate impression of prices even in countries with high rates of inflation. Most prices quoted in this book have been converted to US$ and £.

Contents

Accommodation

In almost all of the towns in the Dominican Republic one will find hotels or guest houses in various categories and price classes. In the tourist centres (like Playa Dorado and Juan Dolio), individual travellers will, however, have difficulties finding inexpensive accommodation. These areas have completely adapted to package tourism. One should not be surprised at the package tour prices for hotel accommodation: the organisers rent these rooms for the entire year and, therefore, can obtain a much better price than those travelling on their own.
Prices fluctuate constantly, due also to the rate of inflation. Therefore, it is less appropriate to quote concrete prices. Dividing the hotels into categories according to price per night (in US $) will prove to serve better as orientation:
Category 1: double room up to $20
Category 2: double room from $20 to $40
Category 3: double room over $40
(Prices are stated for two persons per night)
Particularly in the better hotels, prices are often invoiced in US dollars. On the other hand, in the more simple hotels and guest houses, one must usually pay in pesos. A 10% tax is usually added to the price per night.

Altos de Chavón

A visit to the Altos de Chavón project (which carried a price tag of about $40 million) leads one back into the 14th century. Located only a few kilometres from the luxury resort complex Casa de Campo, one suddenly comes upon a small medieval Italian city — this replica was built between 1976 and 1980. The idea came from the American Charles Bluhdorn, who wanted to develop this city into a centre for art and culture — an endeavour in which he was doubtlessly successful. Meanwhile, his daughter Dominique runs the "Altos de Chavón Centre and Foundation."
Today, Altos de Chavón is one of *the* tourist attractions in the Dominican Republic. In this city, built from coral bricks, one can visit plazas, churches, residential houses, shops, restaurants and even an amphitheatre. One strong point: the complex does not have the atmosphere of a museum, but in fact of a populated city (admission: free of charge). There are "normal" shops and a small bookstore selling post cards and books in the

English language as well. One can stroll through the cobblestone streets, pay a visit to the souvenir shops or gold smiths in the narrow alleyways or enjoy a meal in one of the restaurants.

At the centre of Altos de Chavón is the *San Estanisiao Church.* From the adjacent marketplace, there is a fabulous view of the Río Chavón, flowing through the valley, its banks lined with palm trees.

Also worth visiting is the internationally accredited *Altos de Chavón School of Design* and the *Museo Arqueológico Regional* which has a collection of prehistoric art from the Taino period.

The highlight of a lazy Caribbean evening: a concert in the amphitheatre which seats five thousand. In the past years, the spectrum of artists who appeared on this stage ranged from Julio Iglesias (also a star in the Dominican Republic) to The Miami Sound Machine.

→*Casa de Campo* and *La Romana*

Amber

Amber is one of the most sought after souvenirs that one can acquire in the Dominican Republic. In the Tertiary Period, almost 50 million years ago, there were still thick forests covering the hills on this island — especially in the north between Puerto Plata and Santiago de los Caballeros. Sap from these trees dripped onto the ground, and was then washed by the rain into the nearby rivers. In this way, the "stones" (which actually are not stones in the conventional sense, but are fossilised sap) ended up in the ocean. The coasts of that era have long since disappeared; what has remained is the amber. Because there have been numerous finds in the mountains and along the approximately 125 kilometre long coastline around Puerto Plata, this section of coast is referred to as the "amber coast." Here one can visit the mines in Los Cacaos, La Búcara, Los Higos, El Valle and Palo Quemado.

The amber has a positive electrical charge, that is most obvious when the stone is rubbed. The Greeks called it "electron." The nuances of colour in Dominican amber fluctuate in an unusual spectrum of varying yellows. Often there are also small insects, plants or gravel and ash within the stone.

In the Dominican Republic, amber is often available in the form of jewellry. The largest amber stone that has ever been found, originated from Sabana

de la Mar. It weighs around eight kilograms and was discovered in 1979. Quite often, imitation amber is sold in the souvenir shops. The authenticity can be tested with ultraviolet light (a blue shimmer can then be observed in the stone) or by using an open flame (amber is flammable). Both methods are not terribly practical when purchasing amber. The only other alternative: if the stone is rubbed, then a slight magnetism develops. Even though this method is not a one-hundred percent guarantee, it is worth giving a try when purchasing amber.
Those who are interested in amber as such should visit the *Amber Museum* in Puerto Plata, which displays a larger collection of amber specimens.
The export of amber is permitted.
→*Puerto Plata*

Altos de Chavón: a visit to this city built from coral bricks will take one back to the 14th century

Azua

The full name of the capital of the Azua province is Azua de Compostela. Both city and province played an important role in the country's history: in 1504, the Spanish Governor Nicolás de Ovando established a settlement here. From this point in time, Puerto Viejo de Azua (the old harbour) became a legitimate alternative to its "big brother" Santo Domingo, located nearby. In the surrounding area, the Dominican troops were victorious over the Haitian army in the battle of San José. Prior to this, however, the French had almost completely levelled this city repeatedly. Azua, with its population of around 65,000, can be reached via the Carretera Sánchez and is situated about 120 kilometres west of Santo Domingo. The most beautiful beach in the area is *Playa Blanca* on the Bahía de Ocoa — near *Playa de Monte Rio,* which is also worth mentioning. Also, the beach near Corbanito, stretching about nine kilometres, provides variety. Moreover, the city itself is famous for the beer which is brewed here! A visit to El Número, where the famous battle of the same name was fought, is a must in any travel itinerary. This is especially true for the local residents.

Baní

The capital of the Baní province, this city was named in honour of the Cacique Indian Baní. He was a subject of the Taino chief Caonabos. Baní, in the language of the natives, means "wealth of water." Important for the Dominicans: On November 18, 1836 Máximo Gómez, who later became famous as a fighter for Cuban independence (his former home is now a museum) was born here.

Other sights worth seeing are the Church of the Holy Virgin of Regla *(Iglesia de Nuestra Señora)* and the beaches of Los Almendros, Baní and Palmar de Ocoa (about 30 kilometres west of Baní).

From June 15 to 17 and on November 21, the annual festivals for the patron saints San Juan and the Holy Virgin of Regla take place. Gourmets sing the praises of the mangoes grown in the nearby Peravia Valley.

Barahona

The city of Barahona was founded in 1802 by the French General Toussant Louverture. Meanwhile, the Dominicans have endowed it with the

epithet ''pearl of the south.'' Located by the foothills of the Bahía de Neiba, this city experienced its golden age in the past century. At that time, numerous people settled on the Río Biran to be able to ship the valuable choice lumber to Europe. Barahona is still the most important harbour in the southwest. However, instead of wood, Barahona plans to speculate in tourism. The beaches of Saladilla, Bahoruco, San Rafael, Los Patos, Paraíso and La Ciénega will be developed for international tourism in the coming years. In addition, the coast is well-known for its excellent fishing. It is, therefore, not surprising that many of the residents of the capital, located about 200 kilometres away, have built their weekend houses in this area for these very reasons.
About 40 kilometres south of Barahona is **Playa Los Patos,** where the *Las Cuevas de los Patos* (Los Patos caves) are worth visiting. This area was earlier the stomping grounds of the pirate Cofresí, famous and esteemed across the country. On various beaches (Punta Iglesia, among others) coins and other articles from earlier plunderings were discovered. Scuba divers still search for more treasures in these waters.

Barahona / **Practical Information**

Accommodation: Hotel Guarocuya, Tel: 685-6161, 22 rooms with air conditioning, located near the centre of the city, price category 2; Bahoruco Beach Club and Resort, Tel: 685-5184, approximately 200 hotel rooms and apartments, south of Barahona on the way to Enriquillo, luxury hotel for foreign tourists, nearby, construction on the international airport is underway, price category 3.
Information: A sort of ''Tourist Information Office'' is located at Calle Anacaona 8, Tel: 524-2409.

Beverages

The thirsty in the Dominican Republic, even if they don't speak Spanish, need to know only one word to solve their problem: ''Presidente.'' This is not a desperate cry for help directed toward the president, but is the name of the most popular beer by far on the island. It is available in both small and large bottles. Usually, prices are displayed.
In addition, the island brews two other beers: ''Bohemia'' and ''Quisqueya.'' These are, however, not nearly as popular as ''Presidente.'' Also, there

are a number of other thirst-quenchers in the form of fruit juices. The international soft drink bottlers are represented in the Dominican Republic as well. A few local producers of mineral water and soft drinks also hold their own on the island.
→*Cocktails, Rum*

Boca Chica

First of all: those looking for peace and relaxation should give Boca Chica a wide berth. The capital of Santa Domingo, only 30 kilometres away, has clearly left its traces (by no means are all negative): a portion of a big-city jungle on the Caribbean coast with (child) prostitution, high prices and the typical Dominican problems of water and electricity shortages. The huts housing the restaurants and hotels extend all the way to the beach. It can become very crowded, and this not only on Sundays. Boca Chica is exactly the right place for those seeking action and entertainment.

Boca Chica / **History**

Boca Chica's "career" as a beach resort began in the late 1920's. At that time, Don Juan Bautista Vicini, the island's "sugar cane king," established a meeting point here for the country's wealthy. (Dictator Trujillo was happy with this development, and often joined these circles!) Today, the city has changed from that once in the shadow of the Andres sugar mill, to a beach resort for the common man. If someone speaks of Boca Chica, then he or she usually means *Boca Chica Beach.* The town itself is small, insignificant and is situated somewhat inland on the main road (Carretera Mella).

Boca Chica / **Sights**

Boca Chica's main attraction is its beach. Beyond the almost two kilometre long strip of sand, the numerous restaurants, bars and hotels, there is an extraordinarily beautiful lagoon with water the colour of turquoise. Those who have swum here will understand why the bay is called "the largest swimming pool in the Caribbean." The water depth is at most 1.5 metres. The bay is protected by a coral reef, extending in front of it. Various water sports are offered. One can also wade out to the nearby islands La Matica and Los Pinos. The beaches there are, however, less attractive.

One will acquire a lasting impression of the Caribbean lifestyle during weekends in Boca Chica. This is when families invade Boca Chica with the entire clan, armed with picnic baskets and bottles of rum, cassette players and musical instruments. Everywhere one hears merengue, often played live by older gentlemen. Despite the throngs of people: a visit is especially worthwhile on Saturday and Sunday — in Boca Chica, the typical lifestyle of the Dominican Republic can be experienced first hand!

Boca Chica / **Practical Information**

For tourists who land in Santo Domingo (Las Américas International Airport), Boca Chica is the ideal introduction to the Dominican Republic, and a good place to stay the first night. The city is only about ten kilometres from the airport (the distance to Santo Domingo is around 26 kilometres). Finding a room in Boca Chica is easier than in the capital, particularly since Boca Chica is quieter, and one becomes more quickly oriented than in Santo Domingo.

Accommodation: Las Brisas Guesthouse/Apt. Hotel, Avenida Carrocal 36, Boca Chica Beach, Tel: 523-4316 (not directly on the beach, small bar, restaurants nearby, price category 1); Hotel Caney, Calle Duarte 21, Boca Chica Beach, Tel: 523-4314 (simple accommodation, often water and electricity shortages, small restaurant, located centrally near the beach, price category 1).

Restaurants: There are a number of restaurants directly on the beach, which are all quite expensive. Exceptions: two rows of stands with small but good fast-food restaurants (fish is popular). Very typical, good and inexpensive: the snack bars at the end of the Avenida Carrocal 36, where the beach begins. At some of the various stands (including Chicharrón) one can buy deep-fried pork rinds or Yaniqueques, a type of pancake. Located somewhat further away, but highly recommended because of the friendly service is "El Almendro" (about 500 metres up the Avenida Carrocal).

Bonao

The small city of Bonao is situated an the Carretera Duarte halfway between Santo Domingo and Santiago. Even if one overlooks the sign at the city's entrance, Bonao will stick in the visitor's mind: here there are numerous street merchants with wicker work, ceramics, fruits and vegetables along the streets. This is the visible evidence of this region's fertility. Other than this, there is hardly any other reason for staying a longer period of time in Bonao.

Braided Hair

Only a minority of tourists can say no to the number one fashion gimmick in the Dominican Republic: braided hair. It can be considered a matter of taste, but the neutral observer on the beach will quickly ascertain that the fashion appeal remains limited. The scalps of women who have been so "coiffed" are similar to broiled tortoiseshell. There is not even a trace of affinity, pity is more appropriate because the braids expose the scalp which is highly sensitive to the sun. Severe sunburn is often the result. Therefore, the styles where only the longer portions of hair are braided should be chosen over those where the hair is braided all the way to the

Tinkering on the transportation and certainly not for the first time

scalp. Braids should not be worn too long because the hair quickly gets knotted. The only remedy is then cutting the hair because unbraiding it is no longer possible.
For those who opt for a change in fashion despite all of this: there are women on almost every beach offering their braiding services. Per braid, one will pay seven to ten pesos. Most often, one will have the choice between a number of styles, presented in photographs. Colourful plastic beads are always braided into the hair as well.
The Dominicans, by the way, are not in the least fond of braids. They are far more partial to hair curlers, which are not only worn in the privacy of their own home, but while shopping or strolling along the street as well. On Saturday evenings, it seems that the majority of women fall under the influence of hair curlers: then, one can see the colourful plastic cylinders protruding everywhere from under the locks of hair — a phenomenon almost as common as braids on the beach.

Buses

Those without a rental car, can best travel between the larger cities and towns using the buses, run by a number of companies (the largest are Caribe Tours, Metro Servicios, Terra Bus and Compania Nacional).
Caribe Tours, for example (the terminal is located on the Avenida 27 de Febrero at the corner of Calle Leopoldo Navarro, Tel: 687-3171-6) offers service to the following destinations, at the stated times and prices:
Barahona : 17 pesos; 7 am and 2:30 pm
Bonao: 10 pesos; 7:15 and 10 am, 12:45 and 3 pm
Cabrera: 26 pesos; 7:30 am and 3 pm
Jarabacoa: 23 pesos; 7:30 am and 3 pm
La Vega: 15 pesos; 7:15 and 10 am, 12:45 and 3 pm
Monte Cristi: 29 pesos; 6:30 and 7:30 am, 2 and 3 pm
Nagua: 23 pesos; 7:15 and 7:30 am, 1:30, 3 and 3:45 pm
Puerto Plata: 33 pesos; 7, 10 and 11 am, 1:30, 4 and 5:30 pm
Río San Juan: 26 pesos; 7:30 am and 3 pm
Samaná: 25 pesos; 7:15 am, 1:30 and 3:45 pm
Sánchez: 25 pesos; 7:15 am, 1:30 and 3:45 pm
San Francisco de Macoris: 17 pesos; 7 and 10 am, 2 and 5 pm

Santiago: 23 pesos; 6:30, 7, 7:30, 9, 10 and 11 am, 12:30, 1:30 2, 3, 4, 5:30, 6:15 and 7:35 pm
Sosúa: 37 pesos; 7, 10 and 11 am, 1:30 and 5:30 pm
→*Transportation*

Business Hours

The official business hours for banks are Monday to Friday from 8:30 am to 5 pm. For ministries and governmental offices, they are Monday to Friday from 7:30 am to 2:30 pm. The post offices are open from Monday to Saturday from 7 am to 6 pm and private offices, from 8:30 am to 12:30 pm and from 2:30 to 6:30 pm from Monday to Friday.
One qualification: Because the Dominican Republic is located in the Caribbean, the word "official" carries little weight. Other than the people in the larger cities, not many will be able to much relate to the concept of business hours. What is understood is that "nothing happens between noon and 2 pm." This is when the entire country takes a "siesta." Even the Ministry of Tourism provides accurate information on this phenomenon in one of their brochures: "The Dominican is accustomed to taking a short siesta after eating. Time permitting, you should also try this 'holiday in pocket format' and then you will understand why it is so difficult for us to give up this custom."

Cabarete

On the way from Sosúa to Cabarete, one travels along the Amber Coast, passing some beautiful beaches on which large tourist hotels have meanwhile been built (some still under construction). This is the case with *Playa Encuentro,* a beach which has a relatively rough surf, used predominantly by the Dominicans for surfing. About ten kilometres past Sosúa, one will pass by the Sea Horse Ranch, which offers daily horseback tours into the island's interior or along the coast. Further to the east, the street once more runs along the beach, where there is one bay after another: long, white sand beaches with a gentle surf characterise the coastline, ideal for swimming. Goleta is one example of this. A few kilometres farther, one arrives at Cabarete, the absolute paradise for wind surfers — not only in the Dominican Republic.

Cabarete hosted the wind surfing world cup regattas a number of times. The broad bay, sheltered by a reef, is doubtlessly an ideal place for wind surfers. Experts rank this as one of the five best in the world. The outstanding rating does, however, have its price: Cabarete is not a cheap place — and it can quickly become an expensive form of recreation, especially for the wind surfers. The beach of Cabarete is covered with surfing schools and surf board rentals.
Despite the transport difficulties, those who plan on surfing extensively in Cabarete, should consider bringing their own surfboards along, considering the rental cost.

Cabarete / **Sights**

Tours are offered through the mountains near Cabarete. They go through a "genuine jungle" to a "forgotten cave." The promised adventure, however, remains limited. Other than this, everything else in the town has to do with surfing.

Cabarete / **Practical Information**

Accommodation: Windsurf Apart Hotel, Tel: 571-0718 and Fax: 571-0710, 36 apartments, heavily frequented by Americans and Canadians, not located directly on the beach but on the right side of the main road (when coming from Sosúa), small supermarket next door, price category 2 in summer and price category 3 in winter; Punta Goleta Beach Resort, Tel: 562-2774, 78 rooms with air conditioning, located near Punta Goleta, price category 3.
All hotels on the left side of the main road (toward the beach) near the surfing area are in the price category 3 (between $60 and $110).
Physicians: Centro Médico, on the main road from Cabarete, Tel: 571-0802.
Wind Surfing: At the Carib-Bic-Center, Calle Beller 7 (Fax: 586-1828), surfboard rentals cost $15 per hour, $60 for 5 hours, $100 for 10 hours, $185 for one week and $300 for two weeks. These prices are comparable to the other centres.
From December well into spring, the wind blows here at a speed of about 15 knots, increasing in the late afternoon. In the summer, the wind first

"Fear" reigns during the carnival season when the "limping devils" prowl the streets ▶

picks up late in the morning and then reaches a speed of 25 knots and more.

Cabral

The town of Cabral is located west of Barahona (a side road leading from the Carretera Sánchez) and is known across the entire island for two reasons: the Lago de Rincón (northwest of Cabral) is worth visiting as well as the Cachuas, the masked actors dressed as the devil, who only parade through the streets on Good Friday and the Monday after Easter. On the road to Polo (travelling south) one passes Loma Magnética, a legendary phenomenon: automobiles are supposedly able to drive uphill without having to use the accelerator ...

Car Rentals

Renting a car in the Dominican Republic is often an aggravating and unfortunately almost always an expensive endeavour — despite numerous "special" offers!
Usually, the traveller will find a better bargain when renting a car from a local agency in the Dominican Republic. This option does, however, have its risks: if arriving at the airport at a late hour, the rental offices are often already closed. In addition, one has no guarantee that a suitable vehicle will be available. Especially during the winter months (peak season) there can be shortages of rental cars. Also, disputes arising when returning the car are often more easily handled with international rental agencies because they are also represented in the visitor's home country. The local rental agencies count on the fact that the customer will return the car shortly before departure and will not have much time. If differences then arise, one can only pay the disputed surcharge or risk missing the return flight.
Rental prices vary greatly. International rental agencies charge a weekly rate between $320 and $375 (11% taxes and around $15 per day for insurance are extra).
Local agencies charge about 370 pesos, including everything.
The smallest model offered is usually sufficient for transportation around the island, because these also include air conditioning (an important extra considering the temperatures!).

When the car is handed over, one must inspect it thoroughly. Upon returning the vehicle, agencies often try to make the customer liable for damages that were already present.
A source of income for the rental agency employees: the tank level is often recorded incorrectly in the rental contract or read incorrectly when the car is returned. The difference is charged to the customer.
Very important: hardly any trip through the Dominican Republic by car will not end up with (at least) one flat tire. Therefore, it is very important to check the condition of the tires and whether the spare and the jack are present.
Most cars are equipped with a starter lock to protect against theft. This should be switched on even when only stopping for a short time.
Even if the vehicle was paid for in one's home country, tax and insurance must be paid in the Dominican Republic upon renting the vehicle. One must expect to pay between $100 and $150 per week. Paying by credit card ensures a more favourable exchange rate than is the case when paying cash.
In addition, a deposit must also be paid. In this case, only credit cards are accepted! Cash is only accepted after longer negotiation. For this reason, one should definitely get an internationally recognised credit card for the trip to the Dominican Republic.
A word of caution: almost all international car rental agencies have "inexpensive" weekly and special rates. These rates must be booked and paid for before departure. In the Dominican Republic, however, one often encounters difficulties having these rates accepted. Suddenly, a price increase is asserted, the rate is declared invalid due to exchange rate deviation, or an incorrect date of return is entered on the rental contract so that an additional payment is due after departure from the Dominican Republic. The inventiveness of some employees is apparently unlimited. (Caution: this is also true for the recognized international agencies!)
Those who refuse to pay, face not being given a vehicle. In the end, the tourist will usually pay. In this case, one should by all means demand an invoice (although this request is usually denied)!
After returning to one's home country, one should by all means register a complaint with the rental agency or travel agent. A refund or review of the situation can, however, take a number of months because the documentation from the Dominican Republic is often not forwarded to the main office responsible.

Most automobile rental agencies can be found in the airports in Santo Domingo and Puerto Plata. One can also reserve a rental car when booking a flight or package tour or by calling the international reservations telephone number (toll-free in most places).

Carnival

Every year in February, the atmosphere of the Dominican Republic becomes turbulent and frivolous — carnival is underway, and in many of the towns and cities, hardly anyone remains at home. Traditionally, the carnival is brought to a close with a festival and parade on the Malecón in Santo Domingo. The carnival in La Vega is the most renowned, where the famous Diablos Cojuelos are up to their tricks. These ''limping devils" run through the streets of the city looking for ''sinners," administering rough blows if necessary (every Sunday afternoon in February). In Santiago, the Lechones are on the prowl; in Monte Cristi, the Toros y Civiles; in San Pedro de Macoris, the Buloyas and the rest of the Dominican Republic is terrorised and amused by other Diablos Cojuelos. In addition to the carnival season in February, carnival is also celebrated on August 16, the day commemerating the founding of the Dominican Republic.

Casa de Campo

Where do chiefs of state and sport stars, actors and musicians, the wealthy and those who consider themselves so spend their holidays like normal tourists? — in Casa de Campo. The complex of villas and hotels east of La Romana is among the most luxurious in the entire Dominican Republic (and the entire Caribbean) — and presents itself as a type of independent holiday resort. Guests live either in a hotel, in bungalows or in villas, some of which are beautifully located in a park-like landscape or on the rocky coastal cliffs. One can travel between the individual buildings with a shuttle bus or one can rent an electric car.

There are numerous restaurants, an international private airport, and sports facilities of every type — from fitness centre to polo field — and excellent shopping. However, many visitors are attracted to Casa de Campo by the 18-hole golf course: this golf course on the coast (''Teeth of the Dog") is considered one of the world's most beautiful by golfing experts. Some greens extend directly to the rocky coast; thus, some of the golf balls have since landed on the bed of the Caribbean Sea. The other course (''The Links'') is located somewhat farther north. It extends between various villas and is less risky in terms of lost golf balls. A third golf course is presently being planned.

Despite the degree of luxury and despite the large number of security guards who patrol the 700 square kilometres, guests not living here may also visit Casa de Campo as well as the nicest beach in the area: *Playa Minitas.* In order to visit this beach, one must first pass by the security gate at the eastern entrance to the complex. After about 500 metres one will come upon the clean sandy beach. The water is usually cloudy though, this caused by the surf. Here one will find peace and quiet: peddlers are only conditionally tolerated by the hotels. There is also a restaurant and bar here.

One realizes the extent of the status that Casa de Campo enjoys at the latest when one leaves the complex: police will stop the traffic on the

Not only for celebrities: on Playa Minitas (Casa de Campo) every holiday traveller will get his money's worth

Avenida Central — the main road connecting La Romana and Altos de Chavón which runs through Casa de Campo — for hotel guests leaving the complex by car.
Those who would like to enjoy this level of luxury at "normal prices," will usually have this option when booking a package tour in the Dominican Republic. One disadvantage: tourists who spend their holidays here are usually dependent on what is offered in Casa de Campo and the nearby Altos de Chavón, because of the lacking natural attractions in the vicinity. However, those who are looking for international entertainment and discotheques are at the right address.
→*Altos de Chavón* and *La Romana*

Cayo Levantado

For many visitors, the nicest thing about a visit to Samaná — with the possible exception of observing the whales in winter — is a short trip to the island of Cayo Levantado. And as a matter of fact, despite its label of "tourist attraction," Cayo Levantado does fulfil all of the expectations of a dreamy Caribbean island: white beaches with sand as fine as powder, turquoise water, palm trees, exotic fish, friendly people and the roaring surf. In the future, this idyll might be more limited: The Cayacoa Hotel has stood on the island of Cayo Levantado for years. At present, it is deteriorating because the management gave up operations due to financing difficulties and disputes with the government. This can, however, change in the near future because a large American shipping company is interested in renovating and reopening the hotel.
All that is currently available in terms of the island's infrastructure for tourists are a few improvised bars offering cocktails and cold drinks and a few stands selling delicious freshly-caught fish and seafood.
Boats travelling to Cayo Levantado depart from various ports near Samaná. The return trip usually costs around 100 pesos. Those travelling by private boat should agree upon a price in advance and pay upon returning to the main island.

Cibao Valley

In addition to some of the coastal regions and beaches as well as the Samaná peninsula, the fertile Cibao Valley is certainly one of the island's

most beautiful landscapes. ''Cibao'' comes from the language of the Tainos and means ''many mountains.'' This valley is the agricultural centre of the Dominican Republic. Even Christopher Columbus was impressed with this region. He called it the ''Vega Real,'' the ''Royal Valley.'' During the founding years at the beginning of the 16th century, most of the adventurers came not because of the attractive landscapes, but to search for gold, which was presumed to be on the slopes of the Cordillera Central.
The Cibao Valley lies in the middle of the Dominican Republic and extends through the provinces of Santiago, Monseñor Nouel, Duarte and Espaillat. Among the oldest settlements in the region are Santiago de los Caballeros, La Vega and Bonao. In some regions, the traditional Spanish has endured in the form in which it was spoken over three hundred years ago, especially in Castile.
One can buy inexpensive fruits and vegetables at the stands along the roadsides.
The road from Moca through the Cibao Valley and the Cordillera Septentrional mountain range is without a doubt one of the most beautiful routes on the islands. Suddenly, one has a completely different impression — another side of the Dominican Republic, not characterised by palm trees and beaches: in the small villages far away from the commotion of the beaches, the villagers follow their everyday routine — wrapped in coats and sweaters because it can get quite cold in the mountains. The Cibao Valley is still hardly developed in terms of tourism. At most one can enjoy a drink in one of the numerous Colmados. Restaurants are difficult to find. As a precaution, those travelling by car should purchase enough fuel in Moca or Sosuá. Service stations are rare in the Cibao Valley.
After the first incline up the mountains, one will pass by the restaurant ''El Molino de la Cumbre'' to the left-hand side of the road (open daily from 11 am to 11 pm). From this ''mill,'' in which a Frenchman prepares fresh crêpes, one has a fantastic view of the plains surrounding Moca. Stopping here is definitely worthwhile.
A few kilometres farther one comes upon the small town of **El Camito,** home to the island's highest arena for cock-fights. From here, one transverses the foothills of the Cordillera Septentrional, the Dominican weather divide, with clouds collecting on the north side. After passing through **La Caoba,** one then reaches the ''hub'' of the mountain region, **Jamao al Norte.** 13 kilometres beyond **Gaspar Hernández,** one arrives

at the coastal road to Sosúa. It is best to take this road because the shorter route via Madre Vieja to Sosúa is in very poor condition and can only be driven with difficulty.

→*La Vega, Moca, Santiago de los Caballeros*

Climate

The Dominicans will gladly answer the question which the best time is for travelling to the Dominican Republic with: ''The entire year!" With few exceptions, this is also an acceptable answer. The average minimum temperature for the year is between 18 and 27 °C (65 and 81 °F). The ''coldest" season is from January to March with an average temperature of a comfortable 19 °C (67 °F) in Puerto Plata and Santo Domingo and 20 °C (69 °F) in Samaná. The ''hottest" time of year is in July: during this month one can count on average temperatures of 24 °C (76 °F) all over the Dominican Republic, at least according to meteorological statistics. However, one general rule is valid: days on which the temperatures do not reach between 25 and 30 °C (77 and 87 °F) are rare. The precipitation is determined by the trade winds and the numerous mountain ranges in the island's interior.
As a rule of thumb: in summer, it is dry in the north. In contrast, the south has a dry winter. Despite this, one can still travel during the ''rainy" season because the precipitation usually takes on the form of heavy showers and thunderstorms during the evening hours. Average precipitation: Puerto Plata 1760 mm, Samaná 2291 mm and Santo Domingo 1382 mm. Swimming in the ocean is always possible: the water temperatures are between 23 and 25 °C (74 and 77 °F) during the entire year.

Clothing

By most standards, in the Dominican Republic, it is always summer: therefore, a travel wardrobe of light summer clothing is sufficient. Because of the high temperatures, clothing made from natural fabrics like cotton and linen is best suited. Those who do not plan to spend all their time

Even Columbus was impressed with the beauty of the Cibao Valley: he called it ''The Valley of Kings" ▶

on the beach, but wish to take some trips into other regions should bring good shoes, a sweater and protective clothing for rainy weather along. In the tourist hotels, the dress is sporty and leisurely. Outside, however, one should not wear bathing trunks, bikinis or shorts. Churches and buildings of national importance (for instance: Altar de la Patria and Panteón Nacional in Santo Domingo) may not be entered if wearing beach attire. In the large hotels, formal attire is usually worn during the evenings. Those who appreciate this will enjoy the atmosphere. Those who do not will have no problem if they wear more leisurely clothing.

Cock-Fights

Even before the Christian chronology, cock-fights were held in Persia, China and India. Today, none of the cities, towns or villages in the Dominican republic can afford not to have a ''Gallera.'' Here, cock-fights take place several times a week: these events are not for those with weak nerves or for animal lovers. These fights are between two game-cocks, which sometimes also fight to the death. Artificial spurs are attached to the chickens' feet, with which they can injure the opponent (which is also the intention). The preparations for the fight are quite interesting: the activities are similar to those before a boxing match. The chickens are massaged, rubbed with alcohol, doped with mysterious concoctions and trained from the age of one or two years. Only animals in the same weight classes can fight against each other.

In the arena, it is usually loud and hectic during the fight. Uproars and fist-fights are not uncommon among the spectators because, for the Dominicans, betting is as much a part of these matches as the chickens themselves.

In rural areas, only men are usually admitted to the cock-fights. Unless one attends a cock-fight held especially for tourists, one should forgo taking pictures, because a flash is usually necessary. This could possibly hinder the fighting animals — unintentional manipulation is not inconceivable. Considering the amount of money bet on the fights, a photograph can quickly become a scapegoat for disappointment and lost wagers. If this should happen, one should leave for home as quickly as possible.

Cocktails

For many visitors to the Dominican Republic, the way to a tourist's heart is through the cocktail glass. This is not surprising when one considers that the Dominican Republic has a number of excellent brands of rum and fresh fruit just waiting to be combined in the blender. One should not miss sipping on a piña colada on the beach, served in a hollowed-out pineapple. The most popular cocktails can be had almost everywhere for as little as $2.

Those who would like to refresh their memory of the times spent in the Dominican Republic after returning home, can mix their own cocktails as follows:

Piña Colada: white rum, coconut, pineapple, pineapple juice, crushed ice and a splash of maraschino to taste

Daiquiri: white rum, lemon juice, sugar

Caipiriñha: sugar cane schnapps, cane sugar, lemon juice, limettas, lime juice, sugar and crushed ice

Planter's Punch: white rum, lime juice, grenadine and a pinch of nutmeg

→*Beverages, Rum*

Cocolos

Cocolos is what the immigrants from the ''islands above and below the wind" are called. They have influenced life in the Dominican Republic in terms of cuisine and culture.

Colmados

The small corner grocery stores are alive and well — at least in the Dominican Republic. The entire land is served by an inconspicuous but highly developed and extremely efficient network of Colmados. These shops, which can even be found in the smallest villages, have all of the daily necessities: vegetables, fruit, rice, canned goods, oil, cigarettes. Exceptions are fresh poultry, meat and fish which can only be purchased on rare occasions. Colmados are characterised by shelves stocked almost to the point of overflowing with the sales area arranged almost lovingly. These shops also serve as a centre for communication for the Dominicans. For the traveller, the Colmados are an ideal place for a cool drink, to get information on the local region or simply to have a short chat, especially when they are located along the main roads or motorways. Strangers are usually very welcome in Colmados.

Constanza

Constanza is the name of a city as well as a valley at an altitude of over 1000 metres. Like Jarabacoa, Constanza is known for the beauty of its landscapes, for its agricultural products and for its mild climate. Nearby is not only the geographical centre of the island, the Valle Nuevo, but also the highest mountain in the Dominican Republic, the Pico Duarte (3,175 metres). Many areas have only alpine vegetation — without a doubt, quite exotic for the Caribbean. The Aguas Blancas Waterfalls are also a beautiful sight. The road from Constanza to San José de Ocoa leads through a very beautiful landscape, but does require a four-wheel drive vehicle to navigate the potholes. The same is true for the road to Jarabacoa: those

Street merchants: the selection is often immense ...

who are following a personal agenda should note that, quite often, only a maximum speed of 30 km/h is possible.
→*Jarabacoa, Pico Duarte*

Costa Caribe

The Carretera Mella (naitonal road number 3) leads eastward from Santo Domingo through Boca Chica. After driving about a half hour (a little over 20 kilometres) one will arrive at the well-known resorts of Guayacanes and Juan Dolio. Why these are considered the heart of the coastline between *Playa Caribe* and *Embassy Beach* will remain a mystery to most visitors. It may be because tourism in the Dominican Republic ''began" at Embassy Beach: in the 1970's, it was the officials from the American Embassy who frequented the beach during the weekends, either looking for relaxation or taking advantage of the surfing conditions in the bay. Meanwhile, new tourist centres on the northern and southern coasts have

Roadside fruit stands — freshness guaranteed

surpassed Costa Caribe in popularity. Presently, one meets predominantly American and Canadian visitors here.
→*Juan Dolio*

Cuisine

The first impression of the Dominican menus can be summarised as follows: everything revolves around chicken. ''Pollo" (chicken) is served in the most diverse variations: most common as ''Pollo frito," fried chicken or as ''Pollo con Arroz," with rice and a pinch of chilies, pepper or a different spicy seasoning. Frequently, the chicken is made into soup.
Typical side dishes are yucca, taro, the sweet potato batate and yam roots as well as breadfruit and cooked bananas. Caution: the bananas served cooked can not be eaten raw.
A typical Dominican dish is ''La Bandera": white rice mixed with red beans and pieces of sauteed meat, served with salad and ''Frito verde," fried green bananas. *The* Dominican stew is called ''Sancocho," which tastes best served as ''Sancocho prieto," garnished with various meats. ''Yaniqueques" can be ordered everywhere: deep-fried pancakes. Culinary specialities that have been passed down from the Taino Indians: ''Cassabe" (manioc bread) and ''Catibías" (deep-fried manioc pastries).
With the exception of the tourist hotels, the Dominicans seem to prefer the English style of breakfast. Quite often, one must be satisfied with a cup of black coffee, bananas, eggs and (with a bit of luck) a slice of toast.
In the fast-food realm, the hamburger has not yet established itself; however, especially in the tourist areas, an affinity for pizza seems to have developed.

Customs Regulations

Articles for personal use are not subject to duty. Tourists are allowed to bring one litre of alcohol, 200 cigarettes and gifts up to a value of $100. The law no. 168, paragraph 5 of the Dominican Republic prohibits the possession, selling or consumption of opiates in any form, coca (Erthoxilon Coca), cocaine, cannabis and marijuana. Possession is penalised with a fine of 300 pesos or six months imprisonment and up to 50,000 pesos and ten years imprisonment for dealing.

The Dominican Republic in Brief

The Dominican Republic occupies the eastern portion of the island of Hispaniola (Haiti occupies the western portion). Hispaniola is an island in the Greater Antilles, a group of islands in the Caribbean. To the west are the islands of Jamaica and Cuba, to the east, the island of Puerto Rico. The nearest mainland is the coast of Columbia and Venezuela to the south.

The size of the Dominican Republic is approximately 48,500 square kilometres. In its entirety, the island of Hispaniola is 76,500 square kilometres.

One third of the island is composed of beaches. Santo Domingo (on the southern coast) is the capital of the Dominican Republic. Living in this city are almost two million of the total population of six million. Over 90% of the population are Roman Catholics.

The territory of the Dominican Republic is subdivided into 29 provinces and the capital city of Santo Domingo. The island's interior is characterised geographically by five mountain ranges primarily: Cordillera Central, Cordillera Septentrional (in the north), Sierra de Neiba and Sierra de Baoruco (both in the southwest) and Cordillera Oriental (in the east). The country's official language is Spanish. English is only occasionally understood in the areas frequented by tourists.

In addition to tourism, the country's main economic source of income is the export of sugar, tobacco and cocoa as well as various ores.

→*History*

Dominoes

No hollywood film could better accentuate this cliche. What is the most popular pastime in the Dominican Republic? Correct: Dominoes. Everywhere, one can see the players (usually men) sitting at wobbly wooden tables in pubs, on the squares or simply on the streets playing dominoes. Usually, smaller bets like beer or rum, are wagered, monetary bets are rare. The rules of the game are the same as in other countries — only the enthusiasm is of more Caribbean dimensions.

El Portillo

White beaches, endless groves of palm trees, a runway, a few huts and the inevitable Colmados — El Portillo has nothing more to offer. And it is better that way. In this natural isolation, one will find everything that one expects from the Caribbean. Night life and entertainment is usually nonexistent (one can find both to a modest extent in Las Terrenas, located about four kilometres away). El Portillo is for people looking for tranquillity and relaxation amid nature.

Beyond El Portillo, the road heading east is almost no longer passable. After a distance of nine kilometres, one will reach the small town of El Limón, the atmosphere of which is reminiscent of a western ghost town. On the outskirts of the town, the river has washed away the bridge. Therefore, the road is at present impassible by car! South of El Limón are the El Limón Waterfalls (approximately 60 metres high, can be reached by foot and only sometimes by car). The waterfalls are worth the trip. There is a small beach where the river flows into the Atlantic Ocean near the town. Those wanting to continue on to Samaná from El Portillo should take the route via Sánchez unless they happen to have a four-wheel drive vehicle.

El Portillo / **Practical Information**

Accommodation: El Portillo Beach Club (99 rooms and 11 bungalows): There are certainly several luxurious hotels in the Dominican Republic, but hardly a nicer hotel in regard to location and Caribbean atmosphere. One can either stay in the beautiful bungalows under palm trees or in one of the apartment houses. There are facilities for a number of water sports (surfing, sailing and scuba diving/snorkelling among others). In addition, there are two tennis courts, from which one should not expect too much, and excursions on horseback are offered on the beach. One can rent a motorcycle for about 180 pesos per day. Those travelling here on their own should expect to pay about 800 pesos for two people per night/bungalow in summer and 1200 pesos in winter (this is an all-inclusive price that even includes use of the sports facilities, drinks and cigarettes). A less expensive alternative to enjoy El Portillo and its beach: Nearby there are two private houses, where one can rent an apartment equipped with a kitchenette: Demetrio and Cabaña de los Delphines (both are located on the main street near the airport, despite the location one need not worry about noise in El Portillo, both are price category 3).

Air Travel: Victoria Air/Santo Domingo (Herrera Airport) offers flights between El Portillo and Santo Domingo (flight time: 30 minutes) as well as Puerto Plata.

Beaches: The beaches are the main attraction in El Portillo. There are no problems getting to the water anywhere in El Portillo — even at the El Portillo Beach Club, where the nicest beach extends along a number of bays.

A wide beach stretches from El Portillo Beach Club in toward Las Terrenas. It can be reached at many places along the bumpy road. The *Playa de los Alemanos* is about six kilometres east of Portillo and is not characterised by its beauty, but by its tragic history: a few years ago, a German built a hotel on this beach. After a dispute with one of the natives, he was found dead on the beach one day — since then, the beach is known as "Beach of the German" and the hotel ruins stand as a crumbling memorial.

The mountainous regions of the Dominican Republic: deep green landscapes and a cooler climate

Excursions: Tours to the numerous beaches and bays are the most worthwhile destinations, for instance the Los Haitíses National Park, to Samaná and Cayo Levantado, but also a hike to the El Limón Waterfalls, near the river with the same name, is interesting.
Snorkelling and Scuba Diving: Near El Portillo, there are a number of opportunities to take part in water sports. The most beautiful areas are (including water depth): Las Ballenas (12 metres), Ramon (11 metres), Morena and Patrick (27 metres), Monika (25-35 metres), Dali (30 metres), Banco Bajito (10-20 metres). Lying off the coast east of El Portillo are the two islands Cayo Limón and Cayo Canas, also diving areas.
Information about diving in the entire Dominican Republic is available from: Samaná Scuba Diving Club, P.O. Box 646, Santo Domingo, Tel: 688-5749 or Fax: 685-0457.
Diving lessons are offered at the El Portillo Beach Club among other places. An hour costs between 175 and 250 pesos (only for hotel guests) depending on ability.

Electricity

The electrical voltage in the Dominican Republic is 110-120 volts/60 hertz. American sockets are used. Tourist from countries other than the US and Canada will, therefore, need an adapter. Larger hotels often do provide them, but they are otherwise difficult to find in the stores.
One characteristic of the electricity in the Dominican Republic is that the voltage is often insufficient: power failures and cut-offs are daily occurrences. These can last from a few minutes to several hours. One should, therefore, bring a pocket lamp with a sufficient number of batteries along. An article in "The Puerto Plata News" illustrates the situation: "Most households in the Dominican Republic did not register a power failure on May 16, 1990. But two days later, on May 18, the situation was back to normal. The energy production fell to 540,000 kilowatts, while demand rose to 750,000 kilowatts. The result for most residents was a power failure lasting eight hours.

Embassies and Consulates

In the Dominican Republic

United States Embassy and Consulate

César Nicolás Penson, Santo Domingo, Tel: 682-2171 (embassy), Tel: 689-2111 (consulate).

United Kingdom Embassy
Independencia 506, Santa Domingo, Tel: 682-3128.
In the United States
Embassy of the Dominican Republic
1715, 22nd Street NW, Washington DC, 20008, Tel: (202)-332-6280.
In Canada
Embassy of the Dominican Republic
260 Metcalfe Street, Suite 5D, Ottawa K2P 1R6, Tel: (613)-234-0363.

Equipment

One can easily forego bringing a sleeping bag to the Dominican Republic. One will hardly have a chance to use it because of the extremely high temperatures. A better idea is to bring along a linen sheet. This is true for travellers who stay in simpler hotels or who want to travel into the more remote regions.
During the rainy season (in the north, during the winter; in the south, during the summer) mosquitoes can become a veritable plague in some regions. Even when travelling at other times of the year, one should definitely pack insect repellent. In addition, there are mosquito nets hung over the beds in the hotels. (The natives have their own remedy for this problem: they either eat a lot of garlic, or treat the bites with tiger balsam — this balsam seems to help with every ailment).
One must absolutely bring along a (large) pocket lamp, which will become a constant companion considering the frequent power failures (be sure to bring enough batteries). Electrical devices which do not have plugs which fit American sockets require an adapter. In addition, it is a good idea to bring along sufficient sun tan lotion (with a high protection factor) as well as lip balm.
Tampons are only available in a few stores.

500-year Celebration

1992 is the 500th anniversary of the discovery of the present-day Dominican Republic. For decades, the islands residents wanted nothing to do with Christopher Columbus, they even despised the conqueror. However, considering the expected tourist boom as a result of the 500-year

celebration, the attitude has changed radically (especially that of the people in charge of tourism).
For years preparations have been underway. Sudden historical discoveries are being made all over the island. Restorations are also underway (the colonial district in Santo Domingo has been all but turned upside down). The 500-year celebration is supposed to lead to a breakthrough in international tourism for the government and the Ministry of Tourism. Disregarding the renovations in Santo Domingo, the celebration will mean little more for the "normal" tourists other than higher prices and (possibly) beaches which are somewhat more crowded. The international hotels stand to profit the most from this spectacle.

Flora

In the Dominican Republic, there are 67 species of orchids and about 300 hybrids of these flowers. The best places for intensive instruction in

Beaches, palm trees, the ocean ... a Caribbean dream come true

observing the island's flora are the Museum of Natural History and the National Botanical Gardens (both located in Santa Domingo). In addition to these, there is also a Dominican Society for the Study of Orchids. The complete private collection of Orchids can be seen in the Jardin Orquideario in Arroya Hondo (owned by Gretchen Vallejo de Barceló, Tel: 567-1351).
Important: Plant-lovers, who wish to take some of the Dominican Flora home with them need an export permit. This is only granted if the plant is in no danger of extinction (information and permits are available through the National Botanical Gardens).

Fuel

As a rule, service stations are open until 10 pm. There are, however, service stations which are open 24 hours, especially in Santo Domingo. The unit of measure on the pumps is the American gallon. One gallon is 3.785 litres. The price is about 6.03 pesos per gallon. (However, an increase in price was planned for the middle of 1990 as a result of inflation). Lead-free fuel is often available as well.
The most important man at the station, other than the filling station attendant (usually a number of young men will clamour around a tourist's car) is the Gomero: a man specialised in repairing and changing tires. The island has a relatively dense network of service stations. Only farther away from the main roads in the more remote provinces can it become difficult to find a filling station. However, in these situations, there are can usually improvised solutions: for instance in the Cibao Valley, where service stations are rare, fuel is sold along the roadside in plastic containers.

Haiti

Those who can afford to do so and have sufficient time should take a trip to Haiti. In Haiti, there is still a strong African influence.
Note: Haiti is one of the poorest countries on earth. There is a inadequate transportation system, a lacking infrastructure for tourists and poor sanitary conditions. Excepting the 3-day package tours, Haiti is still a travel adventure and only suited for those who can counter the limited service and organisation with improvisation and composure.

Haiti / **Practical Information**

Accommodation: In Port-au-Prince, there are the following small hotels and guest houses (price category 1 and 2): Hillside, 147 Avenue Martin L. King, Tel: 5-54119; May's Villa, 28 Debussy, P.O. Box 160, Tel: 5-1208; Sourire Magique, P.O. Box 2409, Fontamara, Tel: 4-0644; Villa Bel Soleil, 102 Rue Laffeur Duchéne, Tel: 2-2787 and 2-3147; Santos, 20 Rue Garoute, Tel: 5-4417; Villa Carmel, 114 Avenue J.C. Duvalier Turgeau, Tel: 5-1606. The Hotels Oloffsson and Mont Joli (both in Port-au-Prince) and the Hotel Beck (Cap Haitien) can also be recommended.

Embassy and Information: British Consulate: Hotel Montana in Pétion-ville, PO Box 1302, Tel: 2-1227.

United States Embassy: Bd Harry Truman, Port-au-Prince, Tel: 2-0354 or 2-0368.

Canadian Embassy: c/o Bank of Nova Scotia, Route de Delmas, PO Box 826, Port-au-Prince, Tel: 3-2358.

Information: Avenue Marie Jeanne (corner of Rue Roux), Port au-Prince, Tel: 2-3076 or 2-1729.

Entry Requirements: There is no visa requirement for Haiti. There is also no mandatory currency exchange! However, an exit fee of $15 must be paid when leaving the country. Leaving and reentering the Dominican Republic is also subject to a tax. The following fees must be paid: $10 upon leaving the Dominican Republic, $15 when leaving Haiti, and $10 when entering the Dominican Republic.

Travel Duration: When flying from Santo Domingo or Puerto Plata, three days are usually sufficient for a visit to Haiti. Two days should be spent exploring the area around Cap Haitien and meeting the people; one day should be planned for a visit to the capital of Port-au-Prince. Worth seeing: some of the colonial houses in Port-au-Prince, the ruins of the castle Sanssouci and Fort La Ferriere.

Higüey

Higüey, the capital of the Altagracia province, is located in the eastern part of the island. The name can be traced back to the language of the Taino Indians and means "the holy land of America." For the native population, the city has predominantly religious significance: Higüey is considered the most important city of pilgrimage in the Dominican Republic. Every year on January 21, thousands of pilgrims flock to the nationally renowned procession to honour the Nuestra Señora de Altagracia in Higüey, which is not only the focus of the Marianna cult. For tourists, Higüey is usually driven through on the way to the east coast of the island.

Higüey / **History**

In 1494, Higüey was founded by Juan de Esquivel, the conqueror of Jamaica. Between 1502 and 1508, the region was settled under the leadership of Juan Ponce de León. After various "miracles" were observed here in the 16th century, the city's significance as a place of pilgrimage developed. Today, an impressive procession takes place every year on January 21 in honour of the "sacred virgin of Altagracia" (the Dominican Republic's patron saint). At this time, thousands of pilgrims come to the city hoping for physical and spiritual healing.

Higüey / **Sights**

In the centre of Higüey is the impressive church of pilgrimage (a modern building) and a smaller and older basilica. Both are named "Nuestra Señora de la Altagracia."

24 kilometres from Higüey is San Rafael de Yuma.

From the Boca de Yuma Bay (with a prominent harbour and a number of caves), Juan Ponce de León set off to conquer Puerto Rico in 1508. In 1513, Florida was then added to his list of discoveries.

History

The Dominican Republic only gained significance in the history of the new world on December 5, 1492: on this day, Christopher Columbus (Spanish: Cristóbal Colón) discovered an island on his first voyage in search of a sea passage to India. This island was called "Quisqueya" (mother of all lands) or "Haiti" (mountainous land) by the Taino Indians. Columbus noted in his log book: "Discovered the island of Españiola. The most beautiful land that man has ever seen." The Tainos (the word means about the same as "good") were descendants of the Arawak Indians. They had lived on the island for over 2,000 years in relative peace and harmony. Now, with the discovery made by Christopher Columbus, the turbulent history of Hispaniola (little Spain) began:

1492: Establishment of the first European settlement in the new world, La Navidad (to the west of the present-day Puerto Plata).
1494: On his second journey, Columbus founds the city Isabella on January 2, 1494.
1496: Bartholomew Columbus, Christopher Columbus' brother, founds Santo Domingo.
1502: Nicolás de Ovando becomes governor of the island.
1509: Diego Colón, the son of Christopher Columbus, becomes viceroy of Spain and rules the island from Santo Domingo.
1697: The western portion of the island, the present-day Haiti, is occupied by the French. The treaty of Rijswijk forces the Spaniards to withdraw. The beginning of the division is accomplished.
1822-1844: Haiti brings the entire island under its rule.
1844: The Dominicans successfully rebel against the occupying forces and the first republic is declared (1844-1861).
1861: Spain occupies the republic.
1865-1916: The second republic establishes itself after the Spanish troops leave the island after their defeat in the Restorations War (1863-1865).
1916-1924: The United States occupies the Dominican Republic.
1924-1965: The third republic, characterised by the tyranny of Dictator Rafael Trujillo, ends only in 1961 with Trujillo's assassination.
1963: A military coup topples President Juan Bosch, elected only one year prior.
1965: Civil war breaks out in the country, ended by renewed occupation through the United States.
1966: Joaquín Balaguer is elected President. He was already active in politics during the Trujillo administration, at the Dictator's side. This burden did not hinder him in his reelection to the presidential seat after various political defeats.
1990: It was once again the 84-year-old Joaquín Balaguer who could surprisingly secure the parliamentary elections, with a majority of only 24,845 votes over his opponent Juan Bosch. Not only the opposition suspects manipulation of the elections, considering that Juan Bosch had won the elections and the presidency numerous times.

The tobacco industry has a long tradition in the Dominican Republic — in a number of cigar factories, one can observe the production ▶

Holidays and Celebrations

The following are official holidays throughout the Dominican Republic:
January 1: New Year's Day
January 6: Epiphany
January 21: Festival of the patron saint Señora de Altagracia (especially in the city of Higüey)
January 26: Juan Pablo Duarte's Birthday (founder of the Dominican Republic)
February 27: Independence Day
May 1: Labour Day
August 16: Founding of the Dominican Republic
September 24: Day of the patron saint Nuestra Señora de las Mercedes
December 25: Christmas Day

In addition to the official holidays, there are a number of other, local holidays. Furthermore, there are various holidays from the Roman Catholic calendar; according to the census in 1960 almost 95% profess the Roman Catholic faith. Almost every large city has its own patron saint, honoured at least once a year.

The Carnival celebration in the Dominican Republic is more a state of mind than a celebration. It is celebrated in February, ending with a extravagant parade on the Malecón (Avenida George Washington) in Santo Domingo on February 27.

→*Carnival*

Illness

The unaccustomed cuisine can lead to problems for those with a sensitive stomach. The natives call diarrhoea "Caonabos revenge" and swear by Mangú as a cure. Mangú is a puree made from green bananas. Others recommend eating only boiled rice for a few days so that the stomach has a chance to settle. Polluted drinking water can also cause stomach problems. Therefore, it is advisable to drink only bottled water. In rural regions, one should be very careful. This is true when showering or brushing one's teeth. And: even though it may be difficult, one should forego ice cubes in cold drinks.

Jarabacoa

In the mountains of the Cordillera Central lies the health resort of Jarabacoa. Here, only little of the typical cliche of the Dominican Republic is apparent: instead of beaches, green mountains extend to the horizon; instead of coconut palms, pine forests are found here; instead of hotels like on the coast, one sees cattle grazing; instead of the unbearable heat one can enjoy pleasant temperatures that often lie between 5 and 12 °C (41 and 54 °F) — a welcome relief from the heat after a longer period on the beaches. Tourism does not yet have a grip in Jarabacoa: there are hardly any hotels or guest houses. The residents earn their living predominantly from agriculture. Potatoes, strawberries, apples, vegetables and, most of all, flowers are grown here. Also well known are the renowned horses bred here: Caballos de Paso. In addition to various hikes in the surrounding areas, on which one can visit the waterfalls (Los Saltos de Baiguate and Jimenoa) and natural lakes (Balneario de la Confluencia), Jarabacoa also offers an ideal starting point for climbing the highest mountain on the island: Pico Duarte, 3,175 metres.

For those travelling on the Carretera Duarte between Santo Domingo and Puerto Plata, a side-trip to Jarabacoa is definitely worthwhile: from Santo Domingo, one turns west after Bonao. Coming from Puerto Plata, one must take the road heading south, turning right at the fork before reaching La Vega (30 kilometres). Both roads are, however, not in the best condition.

Jarabacoa / **Practical Information**

Accommodation: Pinar Dorado, Jarabacoa 2244, Tel: 689-5105, meeting point for mountain climbers, small cafeteria, swimming pool, price category 1; Alpes Dominicanos, 132 rooms in small cottages and apartments, price category 1.

→*Pico Duarte*

Juan Dolio

Along with Guayacanes, located to the east, Juan Dolio makes up the hub of the Costa Caribe and is also one of the centres for tourism on the southern coast. Those coming from the northern coast will hardly be enthusiastic. Many of the beaches have been built up with hotels. At some places, it is even difficult to get to the beach. However, due to the number of hotels, there is also a good infrastructure for tourism: those looking for entertainment, night life and discotheques will usually find a broad spectrum of alternatives.

Juan Dolio / **Practical Information**

Accommodation: Hotel Talanquera, Tel: 541-6834, small bungalows are also available, price category 3. In addition, a number of tourist hotels in price category 3 are available.
→*Costa Caribe*

La Caleta

Directly before the exit from the Carretera Mella to the international airport Las Américas/Santo Domingo is the park and museum of La Caleta. Here, prehistoric pottery and skeletons are on display. Some artists carve sculptures from stalactites which are more or less based on historical documents. Those who need to buy a souvenir at the last moment for the neighbours at home can grab a few things here before departing for the airport nearby. For those in an even bigger hurry, there are souvenir stands along the road as well.
There is a small fishing harbour on the nearby bay. From here, boats depart for the underwater La Caleta National Park not far away.

Lago Enriquillo

At the end of the road Barahona — Neiba — Jimani (bordering Haiti) is Lago Enriquillo. Located 40 metres below sea level, this is the largest lake in the Antilles (about 260 square kilometres) and has a salt concentration three times that of the ocean 70 kilometres away. The main attraction of this region are the numerous crocodiles that live mainly on the islands of Cabritos, Barabarita and Islita. In addition to this, one can see flamingos, iguanas and various species of birds. The residents of this area offer boat trips to the western side of Isla Cabritos, where one can observe the crocodiles from a distance (one rarely comes very close). In Jimani, one can cross the border to Haiti. With permission from the National Parks Department, one can also spend the night on Isla Cabritos in order to observe the crocodiles at the best time — in the morning.

Enriquillo is the name of a native inhabitant of the island who lived in this region, later to be named after him. The Cueva las Caritas is also reminiscent of the Indian heritage: this is a cave with primitive paintings on the walls. One will pass by the cave before arriving at the village of La Descubierta.

La Isabela

In 1493, Christopher Columbus founded La Isabela, the first European settlement on the American continent. Today, only ruins remain from the period. Archaeologists have discovered the ruins of a house in which Columbus was supposed to have lived. They have also excavated a church in which Father Boyl is said to have held the first holy mass in the new world. Of course, so many superlatives will be used in the 500-year celebration: La Isabela will be polished up and made easier to reach by public transportation.

Relaxation under palm trees: on the beach near La Romana there is not a trace of commotion

Language

Spanish is the official language of the Dominican Republic. English is usually only spoken in the large tourist hotels, now and then in government offices and in the larger cities. Despite this, one often meets Dominicans who are very helpful despite their minimal knowledge of the English language.
One tip: it is often sufficient to show interest in the local language, the country and the Dominicans by speaking a few words of Spanish — then the ice is broken. Therefore, it is advisable to learn a few of the most important phrases in Spanish before departure and to always carry a pocket dictionary.

Larimar

That which shines is not always gold. In the Dominican Republic, it is another mineral which is even more important: larimar. This bluish stone has become a popular souvenir in recent years. At first glance, larimar has a similarity to turquoise. The stone is mined in the region near Barahona on the southern coast.

La Romana

From San Pedro de Macoris, the Carretera Mella leads 35 kilometres through the island's interior. Level pastures and herds of cattle behind fences characterise the landscape. A stop along the way is hardly worthwhile and one will be glad to arrive back at the coast near La Romana.
La Romana, with a population of 10,000, is the capital of the La Romana province and is a commercial centre for the southeastern region of the Dominican Republic.
The city extends along the banks of the Río Romana, which flows into the sea at this point. A visitor will notice mainly two things about La Romana: the smell and the smoke from the sugar mills, which descend daily on the La Romana, and the afternoon rush hour which starts with the sounding of the sirens announcing closing time. Then the rush begins for thousands of workers headed home. Masses of people crowd at the train crossing, as kilometre-long trains transport the freshly cut sugar cane, and the old busses headed for San Pedro de Macoris are filled to overflow-

ing. Even though times have changed: La Romana is still a city living from and with sugar.

La Romana / **History**

La Romana is a very young city, in which feast or famine is mainly dependent on the sugar prices. The city only began its development at the beginning of this century. The Puerto Rico Sugar Company provided active support in developing this, the largest sugar mill in the Dominican Republic. In the early stages, mostly immigrants from Puerto Rico, Haiti and the English-speaking portion of the Caribbean came to work in La Romana. From this international mixture, the city has retained a certain attraction. In the 1970's the falling sugar prices caused economic and social problems in the entire region. From this time on, the attempt has been made to intensify tourism in the entire province. One result of these efforts is the Casa de Campo holiday complex, only a few kilometres away.

La Romana / **Sights**

La Romana can only offer limited tourist attractions: the *Iglesia de Santa Rosa de Lima Church,* dedicated to the city's patron saint, the city hall and the district around the sugar mill, where some beautiful residential houses are hidden amid the old trees, are among the points of interest in La Romana. At the centre of the city is the *Parque Duarte.* On the northern end of this park, there is a marketplace (where mostly clothing and articles for daily use are sold).

La Romana / **Practical Information**

Accommodation: Near La Romana: Dominicus Beach Village, Tel: 533-4897, about 60 rooms, price category 2; near Casa de Campo: Puerto Laguna, Tel: 567-2812, 100 apartments, price category 2.

Beaches: *Playa Caletón* is a popular spot, especially with the local residents. *Playa Minitas,* which is a part of the Casa de Campo complex is in a very nice location, but somewhat farther away (to the east at the mouth of the Río Chavón). In the southeastern portion of the province are the beaches of *Bayahibe* (tourist activity is concentrated in the Casa del Mar Holiday Centre) and *Puerto Latuna* (a white sand beach lined with palm trees, about 11 kilometres long).

Excursions: From the harbour, day-trips are offered to the islands Saona (110 square kilometres with the towns of Mano-Juan and Adamanay as well as some caves and a lagoon) and Catalina (located closer). Also a possibility: boat tours on the Río de Chavón.
Parque Nacional del Este: This national park, encompassing almost 400 square kilometres, is located in the southernmost part of the Dominican Republic and is characterised mainly by the large diversity of birds. Some of the caves and the tropical rain forest still present here are also worth seeing.
→*Casa de Campo*

Las Galeras

The beach of Las Galeras, with its snowy white sand, is about 26 kilometres northeast of Samaná and ranks among the most beautiful beaches on the entire island. One can drive to Las Galeras via a paved road from

The broad beaches of white sand are among the biggest attractions of Las Galeras

Samaná. Four kilometres beyond Samaná, one will pass by the small beach *Playa Anadel* and a short time thereafter, *Playa Los Cacaos* (Here, atop a rock formation, a luxury hotel is presently being built, which will have its own ferry service to and from Cayo Levantado). Las Galeras lies beyond the mountains Rnan de Azúcar (493 metres) and Diablo (349 metres), which belong to the Sierra de Samaná mountain range, on the Bahía del Rincón and is characterised above all by the beauty of its landscapes and the clean turquoise-coloured water. In the bay lies a sunken ship, around which, a number of fish and other aquatic animals have made their home. Because of this, this area has become a popular place for scuba diving. It has been discussed, whether a second ship should be purposely sunk to create a further attraction for scuba divers.
Accommodation: Inexpensive hotels and guest houses can be found in this area. However, there is also the possibility of renting a bungalow where a larger number of people can spend the night: Village Las Galeras, four bungalows for up to four people, decorated in south sea style (price category 3). Information available through: Fidensa, Avenida Malecón, Samaná, P.O. Box 66-2.

Las Terrenas

On the way to Samaná, a small side street leads off to the left toward Las Terrenas shortly beyond Sánchez. The street ascends steeply at first and quickly offers a nice view of Sánchez before beginning its journey through the mountains and valleys of the Sierra de Samaná. During the next 17 kilometres (it is 21 kilometres to El Portillo) one will experience one of the most beautiful roads in the Dominican Republic. A landscape, in which densely wooded mountains alternate with brown pastures, and on the horizon, bright white beaches stretch under groves of palm trees. Between the towns of Altagracia, El Naranjito and Los Puentes (shortly after these, there is a nice observation point on the left-hand side of the road) there is no trace of feverishness. The village boys play soccer on the streets using coconuts, while their mothers do their laundry in the village fountain; pasture fences are quickly transformed into clotheslines. In the Colmado, one meets with neighbours or merely sits in front of the house in the sun — "tranquillo, gringo, tranquillo!"

Las Terrenas itself is disappointing. A long main street with few stores, dilapidated huts, restaurants and the school; in addition, a police station and a hand full of bars compose a rather dismal setting.

Las Terrenas / **Sights**

Beaches: In effect, the town has only one sight and that is its beautiful beaches in the surrounding area.

Among these is also Punta Bonita, a beach located about three kilometres down an unpaved road which turns off to the left shortly after passing the entrance to the city. Here one can experience the Caribbean in its purest form: an eight kilometre long, albeit relatively narrow beach extends to the west all the way to Cabo Las Bayenas. The kilometre-long Playa El Cozon is also located here, where, with some luck, one can observe humpback whales in winter.

La Terrenas / **Practical Information**

Accommodation: Hotel Atlantis, Punta Bonita, Tel: 566-5941 and 567-5351 (11 very nice rooms; also a few bungalows; reservations necessary during peak season between November and April; motorcycles (125 cc) can be rented for 125 pesos; excursions to the Los Haitíses National Park (350 pesos including meals and beverages), price category 3.

Punta Bonita Resort, Tel: 535-1336, rooms and small cottages, located next to Hotel Atlantis on the beach, price category 3.

Hotel Acaya, also on Punta Bonita, includes breakfast, price category 2.

Hotel Tropic Banana and Hotel Cacao Beach, both located on the eastern outskirts of the town (toward El Portillo, left before the bridge), both price category 3.

The guest house Diny is located more toward the centre of Las Terrenas, price category 1.

In addition, one can also stay in Hotel Las Salmas.

Night Life: Usually, the streets quieten down quite early in La Terrenas. For those who would still like to try their luck: a Frenchman serves cocktails and sandwiches in Bodega La Propone (very simple; on the main street). A similar selection is available in Bar La Tita. Nearby is the discotheque Terraza Nuevo Mundo.

Restaurants: On the way to Portillo, directly on the beach, are the bar El 28 and the restaurant Pescaderia (seafood dishes; nice atmosphere under palm trees). Across from these is Pizzeria Casa Coco. In addition, one can also eat at Cafeteria El Mamon, Restaurante Mami (seafood) and Restaurant El Rincon de la Tortuga (however none have as nice an atmosphere as in El 28). For those who like local colour: on the edge of town is ''King Kong Burger" — serving, of course, hamburgers a la Dominicana...

La Vega

The name La Vega sounds historical and auspicious: Christopher Columbus founded a fort here in 1495. All that remains of the town is the trace of a memory of a period in time that a visitor can hardly relate to anymore. The historical town of La Vega lies in ruins — about five kilometres northwest of the present-day city, which one passes through on the Carretera Duarte. La Vega, the capital city of the province with the same name, has little to offer tourists, however.

La Vega / **History**

During the late 15th century, Christopher Columbus founded the Fortaleza La Concepción here, laying the cornerstone for one of the first settlements on the island: La Vega Vieja. It was this region which prompted the discoverer to euphorically exclaim: ''This is the most beautiful region that the human eye has ever seen!" (This is often quoted by those responsible for tourism in the Dominican Republic and not always appropriately). Columbus erected a cross here which Queen Isabella presented to him upon his departure from the harbour of Palos de Moguer. There is also a legend relating to this cross: it supposedly appeared in the protecting arms of the Sacred Virgin of Mercy (Nuestra Señora de Las Mercedes) during a battle between the Spaniards and the island's natives who attempted to ignite the cross. On the Santo Cerro, the holy mountain, part of this relict (supposedly from the original cross) can still be seen. The city grew rapidly, profited from its favourable location, the fertile surrounding and the promising gold mines. In 1512, the Monasterio de San Francisco was established, which was declared seat of the archbishop along with Santo Domingo. In 1562, however, an earthquake devastated the fort, the monastery and everything else in the area.

Even though excavations of the ruins have begun: one should not expect too much from a visit to La Vega Vieja. Not even the small museum with Indian and colonial artifacts can change this fact. Consolation for the disappointed: from Santo Cerro, one has a nice view of the Cibao Valley. At the end of the past century, the railroad from La Vega to Samaná prompted a new economic boom in this city located on the banks of the Río Camú.

La Vega / **Sights/Special Events**

The previously mentioned ruins of the *Fortaleza La Concepción* and the *Monasterio de San Francisco* are outside of La Vega (to the east of the Carretera Duarte), on the road to Moca. The ''new" La Vega (west of the Carretera Central) has no sights per se, excluding the modern cathedral, the Palace of Justice, the fire department building and the theatre, which, however hardly merit making a stop in the city.

Special Events: The Carnival in La Vega is very well known (in February).

Shrill and exotic: the paintings in the ''sidewalk galleries" are indisputably colourful

Los Haitíses

The Los Haitíses National Park is situated in the southern part of the Bahía de Samaná, west of Sabana de la Mar. ''Haiti" means ''mountainous land" in the language of the natives. This is also a perfect description of the national park: in the rolling hills of this region, up to 50-metre limestone cliffs can be seen everywhere. These have been covered by a dense tropical rain forest. Worth seeing: the dense mangrove forests, the diverse species of bird and several caves, some of which are even interconnected. Day tours to Los Haitíses — the park can only be reached by boat — are offered in Sabana de la Mar, Samaná and Sánchez.
→*Sabana de la Mar, Samaná, Sánchez*

Luperón

A road leads from Puerto Plata through the vast sugar fields, farmland and small villages. The side-roads lead to the beaches of Cofresí (once a feared pirate, now famous nationwide) and Maimón (this was the setting for a campaign against Trujillo in 1959; today, however, it is isolated and surrounded by grazing cattle).
After about 25 kilometres, one will come upon the city of Luperón on the national road number 5. Luperón has a population of about 20,000 and has become a centre for tourism on the northwestern coast of the Dominican Republic. The city was named after General Luperón, who lead a revolt against the dictator Trujillo here in 1949.
The city's touristic significance is a result of Luperón's beautiful bay and beaches, reefs and cliffs and the luxury Luperón Beach Resort, Tel: 457-3211/9628 (luxury hotel with 310 rooms, of these 188 suites; bars, golf course, horseback riding, helicopter landing pad and discotheque; price category 3).

Mandatory Currency Exchange

The situation is not terribly clear: on June 15, 1990, the government put a new law into effect, requiring every tourist to exchange $100 into Dominican pesos upon entering the country. The government's goal was to keep more foreign currencies in the country. Up to that time, about 90% of the foreign currencies spent by tourists during their holidays in the

Dominican Republic flowed back out of the country. This can mostly be credited to the international tour organisations and hotel chains. In addition, the government wanted to confront the increasing problem of the black market. Due to poor preparation and international protest, this law was "tabled" a few days later. Meanwhile, the government has completely distanced itself from this law.
However, be cautious: when a law has to do with the American greenbacks, it could be quickly reinstated. Therefore, one should ask about this before departure at a travel agency or at the Dominican Embassy, whose information is, however, not always in accord with the actual situation!
Such is life on the beautiful Caribbean island of the Dominican Republic: "Tranquillo, tranquillo, gringo!" — Take it easy...

Medical Care

The health care system is not comparable to most western industrial nations. Hospitals are often insufficiently equipped and frequently have inadequate capacity. The hygienic conditions (especially in rural regions and small towns) usually leave much to be desired.
Despite this: many of the physicians have been educated in the United States, and are qualified in terms of medical ability — and they speak English! Most of the larger hotels have a physician on the premises, and most of the package tour organisations maintain contact with a physician on the island in case of an emergency.
In telephone derectories, physicians' private telephone numbers are often listed so that one can contact a doctor at any time. Because foreign health insurance is not accepted in the Dominican Republic, it is recommended that visitors take out a travel health insurance policy. House calls must often be paid in US dollars. Fees vary.
A detailed invoice is necessary for reimbursement upon returning home.
Some important **hospitals:**
Santo Domingo: Centro Médico UCE, Avenida Maximo Gomez 66, Tel: 682-0171; Clínica Abreu, Avenida Independencia, Tel: 688-4411.
Puerto Plata: Centro Médico Dr. Bournigal, Antera Mota, Tel: 586-2342; Hospital Ricardo Limardo, J.F. Kunhart, Tel: 586-2210;

Samaná: Centro Médico Moratín, Tel: 538-2233; Centro Médico San Vicente, Tel: 538-2535;
La Romana:Centro Médico Oriental, Sta. Rosa, Tel: 556-2555; Hospital Central Romana, Frente P.N., Tel: 687-7787.
The most important telephone number in case of an **emergency:** 711. Under this number, one can contact the police, red cross, ambulances, the fire department, civil defence, and the poison centre anywhere in the country.

Moca

Moca is referred to as the ''gateway to the Cibao Valley." It is mainly the location that makes Moca worth visiting. Those travelling from Santo Domingo toward Puerto Plata and who have some spare time should leave the Carretera Duarte near La Vega, continuing to Moca, and from there, through the valley toward the coast.
Moca is the capital city of the Espaillat province, famous for its agricultural products, foremost coffee, which is grown on numerous plantations in the surrounding region. Moca is also renowned for its especially beautiful women. The city can not offer much in the way of sights: the *Iglesia del Sagrado Corazón de Jesús* with its adjacent square, a viaduct and the *Monumento a los Héros del Tiranicidio* (in honour of the ''heroes" who assassinated the dictator, Ulises Heureaux) are among the city's attractions.
→*Cibao Valley*

Money and Foreign Currencies

The currency of the Dominican Republic is the peso. There is a state-controlled currency exchange rate which is based on the United States dollar. In June 1990, this was 7.25 pesos for one US dollar. The American currency is the second official currency in the Dominican Republic. With transactions involving larger sums of money, then the US dollar plays the most important role.
Tourists should carry some cash in US dollars with them. Smaller denominations are better for exchanging and for tips.

In the banks, one will have no problems cashing travellers cheques in US dollars. Eurocheques are rarely accepted for transactions, other than by the banks.
The Dominican peso (= 100 centavos) is in circulation in the following denomination of notes and coins: 1, 5, 10, 25 and 50 centavos (coins), and 1, 5, 10, 20, 50, 100, 500, and 1000 pesos (notes).
Banks will exchange the following currencies into pesos: US dollars, Canadian dollars, Spanish pesetas, German marks, British pounds, French francs, Italian liras, Japanese yen, and Swiss francs. All other currencies could cause difficulties when trying to exchange them at the banks.
Not all banks in the Dominican Republic exchange foreign currencies (this is only possible at the commercial banks, these banks have the permission from the government to do so. To name a few: Banco Popular, Banco Regional and the "official" Banco de Reservas). Although there is an official exchange rate defined by the government, rates do vary slightly from bank to bank. The Banco de Reservas usually offers the highest exchange rate.

The Iglesia del Sagrado Corazón de Jesús church is one of the few sights in Moca

Importing and exporting Dominican pesos is not permitted. Foreign currencies may be brought into the Dominican Republic in an unlimited amount. However, taking these currencies out of the country is limited to an amount equivalent to $5,000.

It may be due to the strong influence of the North American continent: one definitely needs a credit card (especially when travelling independently). This is particularly true when renting a car: payment and deposit on the vehicle are usually only accepted in the form of a credit card. This is also true for many of the larger hotels and restaurants: ''plastic money" as a means of payment is taken for granted.

Important: Those who would like a cash advance using their credit card will only be able to get Dominican pesos and not US dollars. This is commonly not considered and can cause big problems since — as previously mentioned — in many cases one must pay in the American currency!

Which credit card is the best for the Dominican Republic is difficult to say: Visa, Eurocard/Mastercard and American Express are accepted everywhere as a rule. There are, however, always exceptions. Therefore, one should be informed of the hotels' payment policies in advance.

Exchanging money on the black market is strictly prohibited. Despite this, one will be approached everywhere by peddlers. Be cautious: The black market peddlars in the Parque de Colón are infamous. They are known throughout the country for being dangerous and their wealth of tricks. They work in teams — and quite often in cooperation with the police.

Exchanging pesos back into other currencies is only possible under specific circumstances: one must present the official exchange receipt. 30 percent of the amount of pesos on the receipt can be exchanged back into other currencies.

Important: When exchanging money at a bank, demand a receipt. Many banks do not give receipts unless expressly requested!

Monte Cristi

At the end of the Carretera Duarte in the extreme northwestern part of the island is the city Monte Cristi. After the buildings from the original settlement from the 16th century were destroyed between 1605 and 1606, a new settlement was begun in the 18th century. The city, which has still retained its Victorian style in some places, is dominated by the ''Morro."

Christopher Columbus himself is said to have chosen the name because this mountain has a shape similar to that of a camel's back. At one time, Monte Cristi had a significant harbour used in the export of agricultural products. Today, the harbour has no significance — and the city has more the character of a sleepy little town. Sights include the Victorian Palace of Justice, the clock in the Parque Central and the house of Isabel Mayer. In addition, there is a museum where an agreement was signed by the Dominican and Cuban freedom fighters pledging mutual support.
Across from Morro, there are a few beaches. One can also boat along some of the canals through the mangrove forests. Swimming is also permitted. The area has been given the status of a national park. Characteristic for the landscape surrounding Monte Cristi: salt is extracted from several of the lakes.

Music

Music has one name above all on the island: **merengue.** Even upon arriving in the Dominican Republic, this typical rhythm drones from the loudspeakers — a situation that recurs daily all over the island. There is apparently nowhere, where the Dominicans do not listen to and dance to their music. The children on the beach, the waiters in the restaurants, the filling station attendants, the older residents in front of their houses: and none of them are bothered by not fully understanding the origins of this music. From the name ''merengue,“ most might suspect a trace of African influence. Characteristic of merengue are the sounds of the accordion, drums and the Güira, unique to the Dominican Republic. The latter is a metal rasp (those who improvise simply use a tin can) which is stroked with a metal fork. The result is a scratching sound: an unmistakable rhythm is born. Whether the covering of the drums is of importance is left up to the individual musician: traditionally the drum is covered on one side with a goat skin from an old goat and on the other side with a goat skin from a goat which has not yet kidded. Both goat skins must first be saturated in the locally produced rum (so the ''musical“ concept of many Dominicans).
For the amateur dancers, the merengue is distantly similar to the Brazilian samba and lambada. What the merengue and lambada do have in common: they both originate from the poorer social classes and their texts often have a political tone.

As early as 1795, Peter Labat, a French observer at the time when the island was relinquished by the Spanish to the French, noted: ''On the island, dancing is the most popular pastime, and I do not believe that there is another people on earth that is more partial to dancing.'' He was right — then as now.
Some radio stations broadcast merengue 24 hours a day. At present, the following groups, who play an updated and commercialised version of merengue with modern instruments, are the most popular: ''440,'' ''Juan Luis Guerra,'' ''Sergio Vargas'' and ''Los Hermanos Rosario.''
An annual merengue festival takes place every July in Santo Domingo. It begins during the last week in July and ends on the fourth of August, the day on which Santo Domingo was founded. On the Malecón (Avenida George Washington), dozens of bands perform on the stages and squares, competing for the title of best merengue group in the country.
Salsa also plays an important role. The salsa rhythm has Afro-Caribbean origins and was heavily influenced by the Cuban guaguancó dance from the 1920's and 1930's. The most famous advocates of salsa are Johnny Pacheco and Willy Colón.
Before departing for home, one should at least buy a cassette tape of merengue music: the best opportunity to relive the memories of the island.

Nagua

The road beyond Río San Juan leads to *Playa Grande,* (two kilometres long, fine white sand beaches, very clean, bordered on both sides by cliffs, with small restaurants with very good seafood dishes hidden under a palm tree grove.) If continuing farther, then the turn-off to Cabo Francés Viejo will follow after about seven kilometres. There is a lighthouse on this ''Old French Cape.'' One can reach various beaches and bays via the narrow pathways.
Additional beaches between Río San Juan and Nagua: *La Preciosa, El Breton* (with the Cabo Breton cliffs), *Playa Diamante, Playa Laguna Grande, Playa Boba* (on the river with the same name) and the coast near Nagua, where there is a 12-kilometre long, albeit less attractive sand beach — less attractive because it is very narrow and, for the most part, directly

along the road. The beaches alternate with portions of rocky coastline with cliffs extending into the sea.
The island's interior is very fertile in this area. Dairy products, cheese and other agricultural goods from this region are highly valued all over the Dominican Republic. After driving for about 60 kilometres, one will arrive in Nagua. Even before entering the city one must decide which route to take farther. One can either turn left toward San Francisco de Macoris (in the island's interior) or continue on the national road number five toward Sánchez and the Samaná peninsula (along the coastline). Although it is the most important city in the María Trinidad Sánchez province with a population of around 60,000, Nagua conveys a quiet impression and is only worth stopping for a shorter length of time. One interesting aspect: the beach extends all the way into the city.

After a lazy day on the beach a little "action" is a welcome change

Newspapers

Six morning papers and three afternoon papers are printed in Santo Domingo (all in Spanish). Editions of the American daily newspaper "USA — Today" are available in many shops and bookstores.
Two newspapers are printed especially for tourists in the Dominican Republic: "touring," Santo Domingo, Tel: 532-5577 (weekly; in English, French, Italian and Spanish) and "The Santo Domingo News" or "The Puerto Plata News" (also weekly; in English). Both offer information on services and current special events, restaurant and hotel tips as well as a modest number of news articles on the current economic and political situation on the island.

Pets

First, the best advice for pet owners: leave your pet at home. The long flight, the unaccustomed environment and the high temperatures will mean only stress for your pet.

Colourful cheeriness becomes a key word when describing the houses in this country

Those who would like to bring their pet along despite this, must have the following papers: for dogs, proof that the animal has had a rabies vaccination, Parvo vaccination (given at least 30 days prior to departure) and health certification (not older than 15 days prior to departure). For cats, a rabies vaccination is necessary (issued at least 30 days prior to departure) and health certification (not older than 15 days prior to departure). If these requirements are not met, then the animal will be quarantined for 8 to 30 days. The Ministry for Animal Health in Santo Domingo (Tel: 542-0132) will provide health certification, necessary for returning to your home country.

Pharmacies

Those who require medication in an emergency: the following pharmacy offers 24-hour service: Farmacia Dr. Camilo CxA, Calle Paseo de los Locutores (near Avenida Winston Churchill), Santo Domingo, Tel: 566-5575, 566-1253 or 566-3929. Or (during regular business hours): Farmacia San Antonio, Calle del Sol 169, Santiago, Tel: 582-5261 or 587-6446; Farmacia Virginia, Calle 12 de Julio 137, Puerto Plata, Tel: 586-2958; Farmacia Andreita, Avenida Independencia 55, San Pedro de Macoris, Tel: 529-3954; or Farmacia Lincoln, Avenida Lincoln, Santo Domingo, Tel: 562-5147 or 562-5095.

The pharmacies are well stocked, but because the composition of various medications can vary, one should definitely bring along a sufficient supply of any medication taken regularly.

Photography

As always when taking pictures of people, one should generally be tactful and ask permission. The Dominicans usually enjoy having their picture taken, but the custom has taken root in many places that one must pay to take someone's picture. This is true near the large tourist centres especially.

One should be very discreet when photographing the workers in the sugar fields. They have little understanding for being photographed during their work. In this case one should discuss possible remuneration beforehand.

Thereby, one must consider that the workers are almost always poorly paid and usually live at the poverty level.
In some museums, taking pictures is prohibited. This is also true for military bases and zones. In addition, taking pictures of soldiers on duty or in uniform is forbidden!
It is best to bring enough film from one's home country. In most hotels, film can also be purchased. The optimal film sensitivity is 64 ASA since one can almost always count on sunshine.
→also *Cock-Fights*

Pico Duarte

Pico Duarte, at 3,175 metres, the highest mountain on the entire island (including Haiti), is southwest of Jarabacoa in the Cordillera Central mountain range. Other mountains over 3,000 metres in the area: La Rusilla (3,045 metres) and La Pelona (3,150 metres).
Tours of the mountains and mountain climbing expeditions are possible even without extensive mountain climbing experience (usually offered in Constanza and Jarabacoa). Despite this, one should definitely ensure that one brings along quality equipment: proper shoes are of the utmost importance. Tours through the Pico Duarte region last three to five days. Because of the dense vegetation in some areas, hiking can become quite cumbersome at some points. If one takes the "official" approach, then one needs permission from the National Parks Department to climb the Pico Duarte. If one simply starts climbing (with a local guide, if possible) not much will happen.
→*Jarabacoa*

Playa Dorada

About five kilometres from Puerto Plata is Playa Dorada, one of the largest holiday centres in the Dominican Republic. Here, there are not only 11 different hotels (all with high standards in price category 3), but one also has a number of sports facilities available (all types of water sports, horseback riding and tennis), an 18-hole golf course and a casino (in Jack Tar Village). The catalyst for this boom in tourism was the *Playa Dorada,* a clean sand beach, extending about three kilometres in length. The beach stretches along the shores of a large bay. The Playa Dorado Holiday Centre offers a total of 5,300 beds (the entire northern coast has a total of over 15,200 beds dispersed among 116 hotels). The most significant hotels here are: Villas Doradas, Dorado Naco, Heavens, Eurotel Playa Dorada, Jack Tar Village and Flamenco Beach. Important: When booking a room in one of these hotels, be sure to ask about the location of the hotel and the room. Not all have optimal access to the beach. From some hotel rooms one must trek hundreds of yards through the entire complex to the beach. An ''athletic" activity which one will gladly forego considering the hot temperatures.

To offer variety from the beach holiday routine of water and pool bars, tour agencies offer their clientele diverse excursions. Most of these take a full day and convey at least a limited impression of the country and its people. One of the largest organisations offers the following:

- The countryside and people of the Cibao Valley: 250 pesos
- The mountains of Jarabacoa: 320 pesos
- The capital of Santo Domingo: 320 pesos
- Playa Grande and Río San Juan/the northern coast: 220 pesos
- Cabarete with a tour of the cave: 180 pesos
- Horseback tours through the hinterlands of Puerto Plata: 300 pesos
- Tour to the neighbouring country of Haiti (including flight; without exit and entry taxes): $235

Those who don't always want to chat about the weather with the same people in their hotel: in the Andromeda Discotheque (Heavens Resort, Tel: 586-5250), there is a lively atmosphere with disco music, merengue and salsa every night between 9 pm and dawn (admission: 20 pesos).

Police

The topic of police is especially of interest to tourists, particularly those travelling by car, but does not necessarily imply an unpleasant encounter. It is important to know that the police profession is one of the worst paid in the entire country. Then, one might be able to understand why many police officers are constantly looking for a small source of supplementary income.

Tourists are particularly eligible as this possible source. Thus, on some roads, one must push on from one radar trap to the next. In particular,

the Las Américas highway (from Santo Domingo to Boca Chica) is crawling with the "enforcers of law and order," forcing motorists to pull over. Now, a tenacious discussion will usually begin. At this point, it is best to present oneself as ignorant: Non hablo Español, non comprendo Español. Often one is allowed to continue due to difficulties in communication. The "gringo" has a "foreigner's advantage" in this case.
If, however, one has actually committed a traffic violation or if one happens to encounter a particularly stubborn police officer, then the grappling about the amount of the fine begins. At the beginning, a fine of up to 10,000 pesos is up for debate, but in the end the police officer will often give in: "Ok, you can drive on, but how about buying me a beer?" Those who insist on the option to continue their journey "free of charge" can do so without any problems.

Prices

The Dominican Republic must also fight rising prices. The inflation rate increases from year to year. In 1989, it was 150 percent. For this reason, the prices quoted in this book are subject to change. All prices stated are based on the rates in July 1990.

Puerto Plata

On the way from Santo Domingo toward Puerto Plata, one must turn off of the Carretera Duarte near José E. Bisonó heading north. One then drives through the Cordillera Septentrional near Altamira before the road leads back toward the coast in a large arc: after having been in the green mountains of the island's interior, the Atlantic ocean suddenly comes into view, shimmering silver in the evening sun. In recent years, international tourism managers have heavily gilded the name of Puerto Plata: the "silver harbour" has become a centre for international tourism. Despite the intensive construction boom, however, the core of the city has retained a certain flair. Activity is most concentrated around the Parque Central. Especially during weekends, the square with its Victorian pavilion becomes a common meeting place.
Although one runs into signs of international tourism constantly in the centre of the city, the alleyways nearby still smack of typical Caribbean

atmosphere. The numerous Victorian houses, some still in good repair, are especially beautiful.
Puerto Plata, located in the middle of sugar cane fields, made a name for itself because of its harbour and its beautiful surroundings including the Isabel de Torres mountain.

Puerto Plata / **History**

Nicolás de Ovando founded the city in 1504 at the express request of Christopher Columbus, who laid anchor here on January 11, 1493. The beauty of this city inspired the discoverer to name the bay ''Puerto Plata,'' the silver harbour.
Today, Puerto Plata is the capital of the Puerto Plata province.

Puerto Plata / **Sights**

Amber Museum: This museum is located on the second floor of a beautiful house with a small garden and a café on the corner of Calle Duarte and Calle Emilio Prudhomme (Tel: 586-2848). A copious selection of specimens typical to the section of coast east of Puerto Plata (the amber coast) is on display here. The amber on display is between 30 and 50 million years old and includes stones containing small insects, small animals, plants and volcanic ash. The collection, assembled by the directors, Didi and Aldo Costa, counts as one of the most extensive of its kind in the world. The museum was opened to the public in 1982. It is open from 9 am to 6 pm (admission: 3 pesos).
Note: On the first floor is a huge souvenir shop, which already points to an important factor for the museum's existence: this is less a museum than a profit-oriented tourist attraction — it may not be suited to everyone's taste.
Fortaleza San Felipe: Built during the mid 16th century by the Spaniards to protect the city from pirate attacks, San Felipe already began to lose influence in 1577. The decreasing economic and strategic significance over the years accomplished the rest. It was only a number of years later that a use — albeit a dubious one — was found for this fort: it served as a prison during the Trujillo era (1930-1961).
Today, San Felipe is the only intact reminder of Puerto Plata's colonial past. The fort is located at the western end of the Malecón on a small peninsula, where a memorial to General Gregorio Luperón also stands.

The fort is open daily from 9 am to noon and from 3 to 5 pm (admission: 5 pesos). In the fort there is a small military museum and the former prison cell in which the city's founder Juan Pablo Duarte was held captive. High expectations are, however, not appropriate when visiting this fort.

Pico Isabel de Torres: The geological highlight of Puerto Plata is, in addition to the harbour, the approximately 800 metre high mountain Isabel de Torres in the southwestern portion of the city. The only cableway in the Caribbean takes visitors to its summit (adults: 5 pesos; children under 10: 3 pesos). The summit is enhanced not only by a botanical garden, but also by a statue of Christ similar to the far more famous statue on the Corcovado in Rio de Janeiro. An alternative: as the cableway is quite often not in operation, one can also reach the summit via a provisional road. This road is well-suited for hiking.

Cock-Fights: Cock-fights are relatively tourist-oriented events in Puerto Plata. The "Gallera" is located on the Calle Ramon Hernandez (the first street south of the Malecón). Matches take place on Thursdays and Saturdays from 1 pm, and Sundays from 2:30 pm. They last until around 6 pm on both days with about 30 matches. As the arena is frequently visited by tour groups, admission is charged. This can cost up to 20 pesos. There is always the option to "recover" the admission fee: bets are taken at as little as one peso.

Malecón: The promenade along the coast extends to a length of about four kilometres from Fortaleza San Felipe in the west to Long Beach in the east. The promenade, however, has few profound characteristics. Trying to find cafes, restaurants or nice beaches is futile. One exception (within limits) is Long Beach. Here, some hotels and restaurants can be found on a small beach. The area can, however, not be compared to what Playa Dorado has to offer: the beach and touristic infrastructure is rather modest. In addition, prostitutes often replace the tourists in the late evening hours along the Malecón to pursue their trade.

Beaches: Within the city limits, there are no especially attractive beaches. At most, one can go to *Long Beach* and the nearby Long Beach Park. Most activity is concentrated in this area during the day as well as during the night. Along the Malecón, a few small bays suited for swimming can still be found. They are, however, usually not very clean.

Playa Dorada: This gigantic holiday and hotel complex is about five kilometres east of Puerto Plata. Presently, 11 different luxury hotels offer a total capacity of 5,300 beds. The selection of hotels here ranges from the luxurious Jack Tar Village (with a casino) to Playa Dorada and Flamenco Beach to Villas Doradas.

Playa Dorada is also a popular destination with organisations offering package tours.

Brugal Rum Factory: Those who would like to stare into the depths of a bottle at least once and experience that which is a part of daily life for the Dominicans, should visit the Brugal Rum Factory, one of the oldest and most renowned in the country. It is situated on the Avenida Colón between Calle Duarte and Calle Beller. Tours are offered Monday to Friday between 9 am and noon and 2 and 5 pm. These tours are free of charge and include samples of the products: an ideal place to enjoy a Daiquiri — directly at the source...

Puerto Plata / **Practical Information**

Accommodation: Hotel Beach, Puerto Plata, Malecón/Long Beach: very simple but with an almost colonial atmosphere, price category 1; Hotel

Puerto Plata: still a city with flair ...

Montemar, Puerto Plata/Long Beach, Tel: 586-2800, 104 rooms with air conditioning, near the city centre, price category 2; Hotel Caracol, Puerto Plata/Malecón, Tel: 586-2588, 34 rooms, but not all are available, air conditioning, restaurant, terrace with a view of the ocean, discotheque, price category 2; Hotel Jimesson, 41 Calle John F. Kennedy, Tel: 586-5131, 22 rooms with air conditioning, near Parque Central, located in the older section of Puerto Plata, nice atmosphere, price category 2.
Festival: Every October, the famous "Puerto Plata Festival" takes place. It is a cultural and culinary event with exhibitions, concerts, parades, dance and a festive atmosphere.
International Airport: The La Unión Airport (Tel: 586-0313) is located around 13 kilometres east of the city. It is 10 kilometres from Sosúa. A number of international airlines have their offices here (among others, Air Canada, Tel: 586-0252; American Airlines, Tel: 586-0325; Dominicana de Aviación, Tel: 586-0217, and Pan Am, Tel: 586-0227). Flights are available to the various Caribbean islands as well as Canada and the US.

... and a typically Caribbean atmosphere

In addition to various car rental agencies (Information: AVIS, Tel: 586-0214; Nelly Rent-a-Car, Tel: 586-4888), there is also a duty free shop (departures) as well as a CODETEL Centre. One must expect to pay about 50 pesos for a taxi into the city.

Physicians: In an emergency, contact the private clinic ''Centro Médico Dr. Bournigal,'' Antera Mota, Tel: 586-2342 or the Hospital Ricardo Limardo, Calle J. F. Kunhart, Tel: 586-2210.

Police: Tel: 586-2804/2028.

Population: Approximately 90,000.

Post Office: The post office is located on the corner of Calle Separación and Calle 12 de Julio. It is open Monday to Saturday from 8 am to 5 pm.

Restaurants: A number of restaurants offering local cuisine as well as international specialties can be found in the area near Long Beach. Near Parque Central, one can dine on the terrace of the Plaza los Messones. It can be recognized by its turquoise and white roof in turn-of-century Victorian style. Local residents as well as tourists often meet for a beer in Restaurant Central, also located near Parque Central.

Tours of the City: Near Parque Central, the locals offer their services as tour guides of the city. Should you be interested: write down all of the points of interest in the city or a shopping list. Do not be swayed from these expectations; stick by your list and definitely agree upon a price before the tour.

Transportation: Both bus lines, Metro (Tel: 586-3736) and Caribe Tours (Tel: 586-4544), have services to Santo Domingo (daily, four hours travel time, about 30 pesos, via Santiago). Guaguas (small private buses) also travel to Santiago (cheaper). Buses depart about every 15 minutes from La Javilla or the western side of the Parque Central between 6 am and 5 pm. Those who can catch the driver's attention can also stop the buses along their route on the Circunvalación or the Puerto Plata — Sosúa Highway along the roadside.

For the trip to the tourist centres in the east, one must expect to pay the following Guagua fares: Sosúa 3 pesos (25 km), Cabarete 4 pesos (35 km), Río San Juan 8 pesos (110 km) and Nagua 18-20 pesos (140 km).

Tip: The Puerto Plata Beach Hotel also has an adjacent casino (open daily from 6 pm, but interesting after about 10 pm). Those who want to put their luck to the test can play black jack, roulette or the slot machines here (bets accepted from 2 pesos; US dollars also accepted). Those who merely want to spend an inexpensive evening at the casino will not be

disappointed either: drinks and sandwiches are served free of charge to those playing (admission is free). The dress code is more leisurely. One should, however, not appear in swimming attire.
→*Playa Dorada*

Punta Cana

The beach of Punta Cana on the eastern coast still seems relatively tranquil. However, most of the new hotels planned to be built in the Dominican Republic by 1994 will be built here. These hotels will be large, self-sufficient holiday complexes without exception, since the infrastructure is lacking on this thinly populated coastline. The few towns are dispersed among the endless palm groves. To date, the following complexes have been completed: Bavaro Beach (1,050 rooms, on Bavaro Beach), Club Med, Punta Cana Beach Resort and Sandals (all located on Punta Cana Beach).
A consolation: Punta Cana's main attraction is the 50 kilometres long, white sand beach. It extends between Punta Cana, Bavaro and Macao without interruption. Therefore, there is (still) enough space to successfully avoid the hotel complexes.
Higüey is a base centre for the eastern coast. From here, it is a distance of about 40 kilometres to the coast. In rather isolated areas, public transportation operates only irregularly. The best means of exploring and discovering the truly untouched sections of coastline is with a motorcycle suited to the terrain.

Punta Rucia

The Punta Rucia peninsula is located east of Monte Cristi, quite near the town of Esero Hondo. Situated here are *Playa de la Enseñada* and Discovery Bay. The region is also renowned for the diversity of orchids found here. Hotel La Orquidia de Sol, Tel: 583-2825 (28 rooms, price category 2) is the best address when staying overnight in Punta Rucia.

Real Estate

Office buildings offered by real estate agencies have sprouted up all over the Dominican Republic in recent years. There are hardly any more beaches where small plots of land have not been parcelled off for sale. For many, the Dominican Republic has become a Mecca for those wanting to drop out of society. Restaurant owners from around the world have obviously found the right place to settle down for a longer period of time in the Dominican Republic. ''English spoken,'' along with a number of similar signs for other European languages, can often be seen in the Dominican Republic.

The government encourages foreign investors to settle in the Dominican Republic. Among other factors, the Dominican government guarantees tax advantages in accordance with a law passed in 1971. Little thought is given to the negative aspects of the nationwide parcelling of land as long as the US dollars continue to flow into the country as a result of the flourishing tourism.

Religion

According to the census in 1961, 98% of the Dominican Republic's population is of the Roman Catholic faith. Even today, this figure will not have changed much, especially since Pope John Paul II visited the island a few years ago, strengthening the position of the Catholic Church.

Holy mass in English is held in Santo Domingo in the church Hogar Escuela Mercedes Amiama B. 101, Gustavo Mejia Ricart (across from La Baguette) on Sundays at 9:30 am. In Santo Domingo, there is also a Baptist congregation: First Baptist Church, Avenida Sarasota (Tel: 532-4963, near the El Embajador Hotel, services in English, Sundays at 11 am). Although the churches have fought against the voodoo cult and the influence of superstition, pronounced forms of superstitious practice can still be found, especially in the rural areas of the Dominican Republic. Voodoo cults, practising the invocation of protective spirits in every type of situation in life or for every type of illness, have been largely repressed. The situation in the Dominican Republic can by no means be compared with that in the neighbouring country of Haiti, where voodoo is an integral part of daily life.

Punta Cana: where a few untouched beaches can still be found ▶

Río San Juan

The road from Sosúa and Cabarete is mostly well paved. Near Gaspar Hernández it leads into the island's interior for a short distance, through fertile pasture land and banana plantations. A few kilometres farther, it leads back along the coast by a number of beautiful, lonesome beaches like *Playa La Ermita* (dark sand, small huts and simple restaurants), *Playa Ogelio* (off a fork from the main road, the way is marked) and *Playa Bahía Escondida* (about 500 metres from the road; also dark sand; hotel planned, but still quite untouched). About 70 kilometres beyond the beginning of Sosúa, one will come upon the town of Río San Juan, which leaves a visitor with an impression of degeneration. However, only few tourists come to the María Trinidad Sánchez province because of Río San Juan, whose population of 12,000 makes its living by fishing and farming. Those who come to this region will definitely take a trip to the Gri-Gri Lagoon. This is a canal with crystal clear water, surrounded by tropical vegetation and leading past a cave (Cuevas de las Golondrinas), before flowing into the open sea a few hundred metres farther. At the beginning of the canal, there is a small harbour with diverse snack bars and souvenir stands. From here, fishermen offer boat tours through the Gri-Gri Lagoon (boats seat up to eight, prices are negotiated). Other than this, Río San Juan has little to offer and is hardly worth stopping for a longer period of time. Activity is mainly concentrated along the main road from Sosúa to Nagua. For tourists travelling by car: here, there are a number of service stations and automobile repair shops.

The world bank has meanwhile granted two loans amounting to $40 million to develop the region around Río San Juan for international tourism. The first project: in the near future a gigantic holiday complex with over 2,000 beds is planned to ''reanimate" the region's economy.

Río San Juan / **Practical Information**

Accommodation: Río San Juan Hotel, Tel: 589-2211 and 589-2379 (near Playa Grande, 38 rooms, price category 2).

→*Nagua*

Rum

They are the trademarks of every Colmados (and also used in advertising). They are as much a part of life in the Dominican Republic as the ocean and the palm trees. They help the "true" Dominican through the most difficult and most wonderful hours in life: the products of the island's large rum distilleries. The most renowned are the three capital B's: Brugal, Bermudez and Barcelo. (Although many find the brand Macorix to taste the best). The basic ingredient in Rum is a molasses made from the juice of sugar cane. There is certainly plenty of sugar cane on the island. This is the key to success: the Dominican brands of rum can meanwhile compete on the international market.

In general, there are three types of rum: white rum is dry and relatively light (well suited for mixed drinks); brown rum is more aromatic and rich in flavour; Anejos is a variety of rum which is aged over a number of years, allowing it to acquire a particular aroma from being stored in wooden vats (Macorix, among other brands).

→*Cocktails, Beverages*

Sabana de la Mar

The shortest distance is not always the quickest way. This is at least true for travellers wanting to drive to Samaná from the eastern coast (Punta Cana) or the southern coast. The peninsula seems to be quite within reach when driving via Sabana de la Mar and through Bahía de Samaná, but in the provinces Hato Mayor, El Seibo and Altagracia, one will encounter very poor road conditions that will destroy any travel agenda, especially after heavy rainfall. Maximum speeds of 30 km/h are not uncommon in areas where the roads are no more than a series of potholes. Another disadvantage: there is no car ferry operating regularly between Sabana de la Mar and Samaná, only a passenger boat. (Sometimes larger fishing boats will also transport vehicles. These are offers which one should not necessarily accept due to safety reasons.) Therefore, one must decide depending on the conditions, whether one should drive via Santo Domingo and Santiago or via Sabana de la Mar when travelling to Samaná. The population of 18,000 in Sabana de la Mar live principally from fishing. Sabana de la Mar is also a popular starting point for tours to the Los Haitíses National Park, located to the west of the city. With some luck and if one hurries, one can take a day-trip to the beautiful Cayo Levantado near Samaná. This is, however, a tip only for the tourists spending

their holidays on the southern coast. Otherwise one should definitely take more time to visit Samaná and Cayo Levantado.
→*Los Haitíses*

Samaná

Samaná, is a name for two different attractions: the Samaná peninsula (990 square kilometres) is one of the most beautiful regions in the Dominican Republic. Along the coast are the seemingly endless groves of palm trees and some of the most beautiful beaches in the entire country. The Sierra de Samaná rises up in the island's interior with the mountains La Meseta (606 metres), Pan de Azúcar (493 metres) and Las Canitas (463 metres). The mountains are covered with dense vegetation. As opposed to the peninsula, the city of Samaná is the largest settlement on the peninsula with a population of 40,000. In addition the city is a commercial centre for this region and an ideal starting point for various boat tours in the Bahía de Samaná to the south.

Although the peninsula always had a high degree of strategic significance, (the Spaniards had already had fortification walls built here in the 18th century to defend against the French) the region has missed the chance to take advantage of the touristic development like the other large tourist centres on the southern and northern coasts. For many visitors, this is what makes Samaná so attractive: one usually comes across unspoiled origins. In recent years, President Joaquín Balaguer increased financial support for Samaná. An election tactic which was certainly decisive since the residents are threatening to drift to the opposition because of the neglect of the politicians in the "far-away" capital Santo Domingo. The tactician Balaguer had calculated correctly, as shown by the election in 1990. Despite this, he cannot take credit for every development: the road from Sánchez to Las Terrenas was constructed through private initiative and private funding. Today this stretch of road counts among the most beautiful in the Dominican Republic.

From Sánchez to Samaná (31 kilometres) the road is paved, but in a poor condition. The speed limit is only about 40 km/h. One will pass the less impressive *Playa Las Garitas.* Somewhat later, one will come upon Balneareo La Fuente (on the left-hand side). The spring and the adjacent swimming pool are a meeting place for the young people from the surrounding areas. Here, there is a small restaurant and a bar. Before arriving in Samaná, one will pass the airport and a large harbour, located about ten kilometres outside the city. (The harbour in Samaná itself can only accommodate small ships and sail boats.) The last few kilometres of roadway are in good condition and lead directly to the Malecón in Samaná.

Samaná / **History**

In 1493, Christopher Columbus laid anchor on the island of Samaná in the Golfo de las Flechas. Here, a battle developed between the Ciguayo Indians and the Spanish conquerors. Nearby is also the Admiral's Spring (Fuente del Almirante), from which Christopher Columbus could draw water supplies for the trip back to Spain on his first journey. In the 17th century, the city of Santa Barbara de Samaná was founded. Ruins from this settlement can still be seen near Cayo Carenero.

The Samaná peninsula with its spectacular beaches is certainly among the best that Dominican Republic has to offer

The city of Samaná itself was founded in 1756 by Francisco Rubio y Peñaranda, the governor at that time. The first settlers came from the Canary Islands and had to not only cope with the problems of making the land arable, but also with military attacks by the French and assaults by pirates and smugglers. Around 1820, numerous black slaves from the US settled here (mainly because of the close proximity to Puerto Rico). Typical American surnames like "Smith" and "Williams" can still be found. And the English language, still spoken by a few residents, is also reminiscent of the dialect spoken in the southern United States. During the Second World War, the harbour of Samaná was used by German troops as a base for battle ships. The Germans were interested in the control of the nearby Mona Passage.
The saddest chapter in the short history of the city was written in October 1946: A devastating fire lay waste to over 100 buildings. Among these were most of the older buildings in the city, restaurants, hotels and the Catholic church. More than a few suspect that the dictator Trujillo was behind the fire. Afterwards, the "arsonists" became helpers during this emergency: those who wanted a new house were given a wooden house within a few months — Dominican election support? It proved to be of little use to Trujillo: he was assassinated in May, 1961.

Samaná / **Sights**

Coral Processing: On the coast before Samaná, Dominicans dive for the rare black coral. The coral is then cut and polished in the factory in the eastern part of the city (tours available). The purchase of this as a souvenir must be discouraged for two reasons. First, this is the only way something can be done to stop the eradication of this rare and endangered species. The other reason is that, according to the Washington Agreement for the protection of endangered species, importing this coral into the US and Europe is illegal. If this coral is brought back, it will be confiscated and in some cases, one must count on a fine. Other than this, the beauty of the landscape and definitely the harbour are the main sights in this city.

Samaná / **Practical Information**

Accommodation: Tropical Lodge, Samaná, Malecón, Tel: 538-2480, central location near the harbour, price category 3 (winter) and price category 2 (summer); Salt-Pepper Country Inn, Tel: 538-2541, on the road to Sán-

chez, about 10 minutes from Samaná, English, Spanish and French spoken, price category 1; Hotel Docia, Calle Santa Barbara, includes breakfast, price category 1.
Cock-Fights: The Gallera is located at the entrance to the city (toward Las Terrenas).
Excursions: In the Bahía de Samaná, boat tours are offered. One can travel to Cayo Levantado from various points of departure. If one rents a boat on one's own, one will pay a price of around 100 pesos for the ten-minute trip. The price includes the return trip, for which the time is agreed upon before departure. One can (almost) always expect the boat to appear on time. However, as a safeguard, one should pay the negotiated price on the trip back to Samaná. Those who travel by larger boat to Cayo Levantado (group tours at specific times and for a set price, a type of regular boat service) will pay somewhat less, but also are dependent on the boat schedule.
Those who do not wish to depart from the harbour can find an alternative on the way to Las Galeras in Simi Baez, located nine kilometres from Samaná, where the fisherman and boat rental agent Monchin Baez can be found. He charges 100 pesos for a tour to Cayo Levantado with a group of 1 to 6 persons, 500 pesos for the two-hour return trip to Los Haitíses (1 to 4 Persons), and from January to March, one pays 100 pesos per person for an excursion to observe the whales. The Baez family has transformed its property into a small "harbour" which also includes a restaurant.
Various boat rental agents offer tours to observe the whales during the months from November to April in the Bay of Samaná. One must pay around 800 pesos for the approximately three-hour trip.
In addition to this, day-trips are offered to Los Haitíses National Park. The prices are, however, somewhat higher due to the longer distance involved than when departing from Sánchez.
For those who would like to make the water crossing from Samaná to Sabana de la Mar in the Hato Mayor province/eastern coast: there is (more or less) one ferry connection between the two towns operating regularly (information is available at the harbour office). Note: Automobiles are, however, not forwarded. Thus, only the long detour via San Francisco de Macoris (or Puerto Plata) and Santo Domingo or the risky adventure of transporting the automobile with a larger fishing vessel remains for those

driving a car, who would like to travel from Samaná to the eastern coast (and vice versa).

Harbour: On the right-hand side of the Malecón lies the harbour of Samaná. From the small pier, on which the ticket counter and a bar are located (both seem not to operate according to normal business hours), boats depart for Cayo Levantado, Los Haitíses and Sabana de la Mar. The harbour, protected by an island, is also a popular destination for sailing yachts from all over the world, which stop in Samaná for fuel, food and water during their voyage through the island world of the Caribbean. The harbour's trademark is a bridge in the southern portion of the small bay which connects the outlying island with the mainland (open to pedestrians).

Information: A sort of Tourist Information Office is located at Malecón 5 across from the harbour.

Malecón: Most of the restaurants, travel agencies and souvenir shops are located along the Malecón across from the harbour. From the bars'

Dense tropical vegetation: the landscape of the island's interior is a fascinating contrast to the beaches characterising the coastline

terraces, one has an excellent view of the bay and harbour while chatting with yachtsmen from all over the world. For those who would like to try their luck at dominoes: every afternoon, a number of Dominicans meet along the Malecón to pursue their national pastime. Wagers are rarely monetary in nature; usually, a bottle of beer or rum is at stake.
Motorcycles: Particularly because of the sometimes poor road conditions, the motorcycle is certainly the best means of transportation when exploring the peninsula. Even the more isolated beaches can be reached by motorcycle. For those who would prefer to avoid the poor roads: in many places, the local residents simply drive their motorcycles along the beach — this is safer and faster. Motorcycles (125 cc, trail bikes) can usually be rented in the larger hotels (for instance: El Portillo Beach Club/El Portillo and Atlantis/Las Terrenas) or at some of the car rental agencies in Samaná (along the Malecón).
Night Life: In the centre of Samaná, the locals usually meet in the Cielo discotheque, or they will enjoy a glass of rum in the El Coco Bar.
Refugees: The harbour of Samaná is frequently a starting point for attempts to flee the Dominican Republic. These attempts are usually made by Caribbeans and Chinese. The goal of these illegal border crossings is the nearby island of Puerto Rico, which is an American possession. For this reason, one does not need a visa nor even a passport when continuing from Puerto Rico to the American mainland. Thus the North American continent seems within reach. The crossing takes about 24 hours and costs 3000 pesos. The ships frequently run into difficulties at sea and many are lost forever in the tides of the Caribbean. Therefore, a possible short trip to Puerto Rico using these ships can only be unconditionally discouraged!
Travel Agency: The Canadian Kim Beddall runs a small agency with the name "Whales Samaná," which specialises in tours to observe the whales. The agency is located along the Malecón near the harbour. It is, however, usually only open during the whale season, during the winter months.
→Cayo Levantado, Las Galeras, Las Terrenas, Los Haitíses, Sánchez, Whales

Sánchez

A few kilometres beyond Nagua, the wooded mountains of the Samaná peninsula already appear on the horizon behind the broad Bahía

Escocesa. Despite this, it is still 33 kilometres to Sánchez, the ''gate to the peninsula.'' Before reaching the city, one will pass by the Monte Las Canitas (463 metres) on the left side of the road. At the turn of the century, Sánchez was the terminal station for the first railway in the Dominican Republic. This was built by the Scotsman Baird and connected the cities of La Vega and San Francisco de Macoris with Sánchez. What remains is only a portion of a nostalgic memory: on the harbour, one can still see the last sections of track and a few benches as they rust in the sun. Nearby, there is also supposed to be a rusting locomotive. Sánchez is, on the other hand, very proud of the fact that the island's first bank was founded and built here. The building is also near the small park along the harbour.

Sánchez / **Practical Information**

Accommodation: Along the Calle Duarte are some guest houses and hotels (Hotel/Cafeteria La Risuena and Barra Hotel/La Gran Parada, among others), which, however, are all very simple and for the most part do not convey a very clean impression (most in price category 1).

Calle Duarte: The main street in Sánchez begins at the entry to the city, turning off of the national street number 5 (toward Samaná) and going all the way down to the Bahía de Samaná. In the northern portion of this city is the stand for Guaguas, departing for Las Terrenas and Samaná. On the street, there are peddlers offering a number of goods. In the side streets, small markets can be found, which sell fresh fruit and vegetables, fish and meat.

Excursions: On the opposite shores of the Bahía de Samaná is the Los Haitíses National Park. Not all of the fishermen have permission to dock at the park. From Sánchez, the best alternative is offered by the Frenchman Michel. He runs the restaurant ''Las Malvinas'' on the harbour. He charges $40 for the approximately one-hour trip. In addition to the national park (mainly various species of birds can be seen here), the boat also docks at a small fishing village.

Tip: Those who would like to take photographs within the Los Haitíses National Park should definitely bring along a flash. The dense tropical vegetation allows hardly any sun through the foliage. There is also a number of caves which can be visited.

San Cristóbal

The Dominican Republic also had its own "gold fever." At the end of the 15th century, the discovery of gold along the Río Haina caused an uproar. Today, the city of San Cristóbal, with its population of 130,000, extends along these banks. The city of San Cristóbal is the capital of the San Cristóbal province, the largest province in the Dominican Republic. San Cristóbal — the name was given to the city by the Spaniards in reference to Saint Christopher, when they built a fort to house the gold discovered in the area — can be easily explored on a day-trip, only 30 kilometres from the capital of Santo Domingo.

Worth seeing is the city hall, where in 1844, the first constitution of the republic was signed, the Pater Ayala Church, dating back to the 19th century and the San Cristóbal church, where one will stumble on the traces of the real point of interest in this city: these attractions are, however, dubious to many because they are associated with the general Dr. Rafael Leonidas Trujillo Molina (Trujillo for short). In 1891, the dictator, who set the entire country into a state of fear and anxiety between 1930 and 1961, was born here. The tomb of the general is in the San Cristóbal Church. Across the street, there is a memorial marking Trujillo's birthplace. The actual house is no longer in existence. More "memorabilia": the Castillo del Cerro is perched atop a small hill overlooking the city. It was built in the 1950's, is six stories high and each room is decorated in a different style. Associated with this building are numerous legends and rumours in regard to Trujillo's lifestyle. They all have one thing in common: they document the inhumane lifestyle of the dictator and simultaneously emphasize his addiction to luxury which he developed at the cost of the populace. Casa Caoba (Mahogany House) was his country residence, where many of the General's personal articles can be seen. Nearby is La Toma, Trujillo's private bath.

A number of beaches can be easily reached from San Cristóbal including Najayo (to the south) and Palenque (to the east). Off this portion of coastline, some French galleons were sunk at the beginning of the 19th century. They might possibly contain some type of treasure for scuba divers. At least they have a fascinating effect on the divers.

The nicest view of the region and of the nearby capital of Santo Domingo is from Cambita-Garabitas, which lies in the foothills of the Cordillera Central.

San Francisco de Macoris

The city of San Francisco de Macoris is in the northeastern portion of the island and is surrounded by fertile pasture land and numerous rice fields. Earlier, the train from La Vega to Sánchez passed this city. The tracks have, for the most part disappeared. What remains is, however, the significance set forth by this means of transportation: if one turns right off the Carretera Duarte beyond Bonao, one can then drive via San Francisco de Macoris to the coastal town of Nagua and continue from there to Samaná.
The wealth of this city is foremost a result of the fertile surroundings. It is no coincidence that this city is referred to as the "Mercedes Benz" of the Dominican Republic. The carnival in February is definitely worth experiencing first-hand.
→*Carnival*

San Pedro de Macoris

The city of San Pedro de Macoris counts as one of the most beautiful towns on the southern coast. In the narrow alleyways in the city's centre, one will encounter a typical Caribbean atmosphere. The merchants peddlers selling lottery tickets and shoe shines have set up their stands near the Parque Duarte. Next to these are the horse carriages characteristic of San Pedro de Macoris. Those who wish to do so can explore the city using this means of transportation. Outside of the centre of the city, there is, however, little worth seeing. The colourful facades of the city gleam in the evening sun; people meet in the pubs after a days work for a chat and a beer. The conversations revolve around one topic especially, exactly as they did many years ago: sugar. Despite all of the problems associated with this topic, sugar is still the main source of income for the populace. The city is located among vast fields, on which sugar cane is grown without exception. In the nearby areas alone, there are six sugar mills, which process the harvested canes — and quite often, an unmistakable odour spreads over the city.

San Pedro de Macoris / **History**

San Pedro de Macoris was founded in the 19th century by Spanish immigrants who had fled from Cuba. They also brought the knowledge of sugar cane cultivation with them. The city flourished in the period after the First World War until 1930. Even today, this historical phase is called ''Danza de los Milliones,'' the dance of the millions. A number of Europeans also pitched their tents here. In San Pedro de Macoris, the sweet life blossomed in such a way that the city could even provide competition for Santo Domingo. The reason for this was quite simple: the sugar, which at this time could be sold internationally at a high price. During this time, it was even lucrative for Pan American Airlines to open a route between San Pedro de Macoris and the United States.

The populace enjoyed life — and built: Reminders of this time are the fire department building, the post office building, or the Iglesia San Pedro Apostól, located on the banks of the Río Higuamo.

Meanwhile, the price for sugar has fallen to a critical point, which has fuelled a recession in San Pedro de Macoris as well. For this reason, the attempt is being made to secure other sources of income by building an industrial free-trade zone outside the city. The Universidad Central del Este with a medical school respected nationwide is also located in San Pedro de Macoris.

San Pedro de Macoris / **Sights**

As is the case in most cities on the island, historical and architectural points of interest are rare. A short visit to the Iglesia San Pedro Apostól church will prove worthwhile. The facade of this church can be already seen from quite a distance upon crossing the Río Higuamo Bridge when approaching the city from Santo Domingo. After crossing the bridge, one should keep right at the traffic junction, and at the end of the street, one will arrive at the church. This is a good starting point to begin one's explorations into the adjacent inner city.

Particularly the Parque Duarte is pulsing with life. Another ''attraction,'' however, can no longer be seen in action: the baseball players of this city — who have meanwhile become famous. Although it happens repeatedly that big stars of this typically American sport originate from here, the residents end up seeing them for only a short time. If a player is good, then he will go to the professional leagues in the United States because that is where the big money is for Dominican baseball players, who usually come from more modest backgrounds. The best players and the most clever American buyers can be found in the Tetelo Vargas Stadium, where the team ''Estrellas Orientales" plays baseball regularly. A beach can be found to the east, the *Playa del Soco,* near the Soco River and the Río Cumayasa is a river popular with anglers. Both can be found east of San Pedro de Macoris on the road to La Romana. Otherwise, the beaches of Costa Caribe (Juan Dolio and Guayacanes) are considered the regional resort areas for the tourists of San Pedro.

San Pedro de Macoris / **Practical Information**

Restaurants: Near the Parque Duarte is the Pizzeria La Lata, Calle Sánchez/corner of Anacaona Moscoso, Tel: 526-6214. In this restaurant, not only pizzas are available, but fresh fruit juices, good sandwiches and a lot of information as well because the employees and neighbours meet in the outdoor restaurant to chat under the straw roof.

Santiago de los Caballeros

In the northern portion of the Dominican Republic on the Highway Carretera Duarte is the city of Santiago de los Caballeros (referred to as follows — which is also the case on the island itself — as Santiago for short). 155 kilometres from Santo Domingo and 69 kilometres from Puerto Plata, this city has developed into one of the islands most important junctions for transportation. Santiago, the second largest city on the island, has a population of 400,000. For many of the island's residents, Santiago is the ''secret" capital of the Dominican Republic: the flair of this city is highly valued; the open-mindedness and the mentality of the people as well. For tourists, however, this city will prove to be less attractive, only worth stopping for a shorter break on the trip from the northern coast to the southern (or vice versa). It does, nevertheless, make an ideal starting point for investigating the Cibao Valley. Santiago has been given the epithet ''the home of rum and tobacco" — two products which have made the city famous beyond the shores of the island. The name Santiago is internationally recognized, especially because of its cigar factories. Furthermore, Santiago is regarded as the home of merengue, the typical music of the island.

Santiago / **History**

Bartholomew Columbus founded this city in 1504, on the banks of the Río Yaque del Norte in the Jacagua region, at the order of his older brother Christopher. This city's beginnings, located a few kilometres away from the present-day city of Santiago, were completely destroyed in 1562 by a severe earthquake, however. A new start was already made in 1563. During the various wars of the 19th century, Santiago, the city in which the most Dominican presidents were born, was repeatedly devastated.

Santiago / **Sights**

Calle del Sol: This is the main commercial street in Santiago (numerous restaurants and shops) which runs from Monumento to the banks of the Río Yaque, where it ends in a rather dirty harbour district.

Carnival: Carnival is celebrated in February and August in Santiago in accordance with the local traditions. The festivities are focussed around the Lechones (devils, whose costumes are decorated with pieces of mirror and other ornaments).

Catedral de Santiago de Apostól: This cathedral, built in neoclassic and Gothic architecture is located near the Parque Duarte and was built from 1868 to 1895. It was extensively restored in 1990 and is still renowned for its mahogany altar.

Monumento a los Heroes de la Restauración: The trademark of Santiago is perched on a hill overlooking the city and points the way toward the city's centre for travellers. As is the case so often in the Dominican Republic: this "architectural work of art" can be accredited to the island's dictator Trujillo. The interior of "El Monumento" is decorated with frescoes by the Spanish artist Vela Zanetti, whose artistic talent has also graced the United Nations Building in New York.

Museo Folklórico Tomás Morel: The extensive collection of folklore artifacts and carnival masks is especially worth mentioning.

Parque Duarte: In the inner city on the Calle Escalante, this square is the focal point of Santiago. Shoe-shine stands and peddlers selling lottery tickets have set up shop here just as the numerous horse-drawn carriages offering tours of the city (albeit a less recommendable attraction considering the hectic, big city atmosphere in Santiago).

Tobacco Museum: Santiago is also famous for its tobacco. It is then not surprising that there is a museum here dedicated to these products. It

is located in the El Centro district on Calle 30 de Marzo, south of Calle del Sol. In addition to presenting information on the various types of tobaccos and the cultivation process, the manual production of cigars is demonstrated here; or shall we say, the attempt is made. The museum is usually closed and no one seems to be able to give information on the exact times it is open.
Universidad Católica Madre y Maestra: One of the most widely known and accredited universities in the Dominican Republic.

Santiago / **Practical Information**

Accommodation: Santiago Camino Real, Calle El Sol, Tel: 583-4361, centrally located, 72 rooms, price category 2; Hotel Matum y Casino, Tel: 582-3107, price category 2; Hotel Don Diego, Tel: 582-7186, 36 rooms with air conditioning, price category 2; Hotel Mercedes, Calle 30 de Marzo 18, Tel: 583-1171, located centrally near Parque Duarte, somewhat loud, simply furnished, price category 2.
→*Cibao Valley, Tobacco*

The Torre del Homenaje in Santiago: the flags of seven different nations heve been flown from this tower

Santo Domingo

Santo Domingo, the capital of the Dominican Republic, is not for people with weak nerves. Those who are looking for a tranquil, idyllic setting should give this metropolis of 1.8 million a wide berth. Some glamour is added to the city by calling it ''the first capital of the new world.“ Until one arrives in the centre of the city, one must pass through vast, mostly very poor suburbs. The centre itself also leaves the impression of decay in some places. However, together with its chaotic traffic, this makes up part of Santo Domingo's flair. To gain distance to this hectic atmosphere, one should take a long walk through the colonial district, which will have been polished up by the 500-year anniversary of the discovery of the Dominican Republic in 1992.

Santo Domingo / **History**

The city of Santo Domingo was founded on August 4, 1496 (historians consider this date to be the most probable along with 1498) by Bartholomew Columbus (Spanish: Bartolomé Colón), the brother of Christopher Columbus. Later, Nicolás de Ovando, Governor of Hispaniola furthered the city's development. He is also considered the architect of the present-day colonial district. The city rapidly won significance and influence: in 1504, it became the seat of the bishop; in 1509, Diego Columbus (the son of the discoverer Christopher) came to Santo Domingo as the Spanish viceroy; the city was declared the capital of the viceroyal empire of New Spain a short time later. The city had to endure heavy damage twice in its history: in 1596, it was Sir Francis Drake who plundered Santo Domingo; in 1930, a severe hurricane devastated the city.

Santo Domingo / **Sights**

Visitors should not place all too high expectations on the city of Santo Domingo. As is the case with other cities on the island, Santo Domingo does have a long and, in part, glorious past, but what is left of the memory of this time is little and what does remain increasingly falls victim to the bustle of modern life. The situation might have changed for the better in light of the extensive restoration projects which encourage an appreciation of the traditional values *(→ 500-year celebration).*

One exception to the general situation in Santo Domingo is, however, the colonial district focussing on the Calle Las Damas. In and around this

district are the most points of interest in the city. The name of this street comes from the period of María de Toledo, the wife of Diego Columbus. Earlier, she and her ladies in waiting would promenade over the bumpy cobblestones every afternoon. According to malicious rumours, they were on the outlook for men as their husbands were sailing the world's oceans most of the time on their expeditions.
In the middle of 1990, however, this street was one large construction zone. Everywhere, the attempt was being made to refurbish the city as close as possible to the historical plans. The background: in 1992, the Dominican Republic will celebrate the 500-year anniversary of its discovery by Christopher Columbus on December 5, 1492. And Santo Domingo, which lays claim to the superlative ''the oldest city founded by Europeans in the new world,'' will celebrate the 500-year anniversary of the founding of the city itself in 1998 — officially this date is 1998, although many historical aspects point to 1996 as the year of the city's establishment. Nevertheless, these are two motivational factors for polishing up the city. One can only hope that the construction work will be completed on time — punctuality, as many Dominicans themselves claim — cannot always be expected on the island.
Santo Domingo has a horizontal layout, which has long since lapped over its natural borders (the rivers Ozama to the east, Haina to the west and Isabela to the north). Meanwhile, the city has grown to the second largest metropolis in the Caribbean (behind Cuba's Havana).
The following **Suggested Routes** can be considered general guidelines for a sightseeing trip through the city on foot:
- from the Botanical Gardens to Mirador Park and the George Washington Statue (in the western portion of the city)
- from the George Washington Statue to the cathedral (the colonial Santo Domingo)
- from Parque Independencia to the Botanical Gardens
- from the marketplace to Los Tres Ojos, and
- from Parque Independencia to Boca de Nigua

the most beautiful buildings are without a doubt on the Calle las Damas in the so-called colonial zone.
The **Sights on the Calle las Damas** individually (from the southern harbour region to the northern Alcázar de Colón):
Fortaleza Ozama: In a fortress system including several buildings, the fort was the most important component. Located directly at the mouth of the

Río Ozama on the Caribbean coast, this fort served as a bastion protecting Santo Domingo from the frequent pirate attacks. Earlier, the fort was called "La Fuerza" for short. Today, the Fortaleza Ozama is surrounded by a small park, from which there is a nice view of portions of the harbour and the lively boat traffic on the river. At the entrance, one passes the portal dating back to the 18th century.

Torre del Homenaje: the tower of homage is the focal point of the Fortaleza Ozama. This construction was built from 1502 to 1507, commissioned by Nicolás de Ovando. In the course of the centuries, the flags of seven different nations were flown from this tower. An adage from Pater Vásquez is often quoted: "Yesterday, I was born a Spaniard; in the afternoon, I was French; during the night, Ethiopian. Today I was informed that I am an Englishman. I don't know what will become of me..."

An interesting occurrence within the fortress walls: the triumphant and pompous arrival of Diego Columbus on July 9, 1509. In the forecourt of the plaza is a statue of Gonzalo Fernández de Oviedo who wrote "The General and Natural History of the West Indies" in 1533.

Casas de Bastidas: Rodrigo de Bastidas, the founder of Coro, the first capital of Venezuela, and the Colombian city of Santa Maria, was made honorary citizen of Santo Domingo in 1512. He was one of the most influential and wealthiest citizens of the city. In the former residence, named after him, there are various cultural institutions and shops today. It is considered one of the most beautiful colonial buildings in the city and is situated near the Fortaleza.

Hostal Nicolás de Ovando: Characteristic of this building named after the governor and founder of the city Nicolás de Ovando is the Gothic-Isabellinean portal. Built in the 16th century, a beautiful hotel with a lavish ambiance has been established within these thick walls. The complexly built house with a swimming pool, still radiates much of the same atmosphere as it did in years gone by. From the hotel terrace, there is a beautiful view of the Río Ozama and the harbour, which lies below the colonial zone.

Panteón Nacional: the former Jesuit monastery was built in 1714. Later this was used as a theatre at times and a royal tobacco warehouse before it was transformed into the national hall of honour under the dictator Trujillo in 1958. It stands out because of its very sober facade. Today, the last remains of various national heroes and freedom fighters are kept here. The eternal flame burns in their honour. The nave and the chapels make up a cross with a dome where they come together. Hung here is a massive chandelier which the Spanish General Franco presented to his Dominican "colleague": a present from dictator to dictator so to say. Not proven, but possible: the iron doors are said to originate from a Nazi concentration camp.

Open daily from 10 am to 5 pm (admission is free; tours are offered).

Capilla Nuestra Señora de los Remedios: "The Chapel of the Holy Virgin of Healing" is also known as "The Church of the Dávila Family" because it was built by the former city councilman Francisco de Dávila in the 16th century. This church was completed before the cathedral and is considered one of the most romantic churches in the country. This is the only building in the colonial district that was both a church and a fortress.

The Sundial: Constructed by Francisco Rubio de Peñaranda in 1753, this is one of the oldest sundials of its kind still in existence in the world. Supposedly, it has never been repaired — and despite this it still shows the exact hour: the Dominican answer to Swiss precision.

Even a viceroy has high domestic standards: Diego Columbus once resided in Alcázar in Santo Domingo

Casas Reales: These buildings housed the colonial governmental offices for over three centuries. The royal buildings are located across the street from the sundial. On April 5, 1511, the Royal Court, ''Real Audiencia,'' was founded here by royal decree. Its jurisdiction was supposed to span the entire new world. Later, the seat of the governor was located here. A unique aspect: on the southern side of the buildings (along the Calle Mercedes) is the coat of arms of Queen Joanna of Castile. She acquired the epithet ''the insane'' when she lost her mind after the death of her husband Philip. In the buildings today, there is a museum displaying articles salvaged from sunken ships off of the Dominican coast as well as pieces relating to the colonial history.
Open from 9:30 am to 5 pm.
El Alcázar de Colón: Even a viceroy likes to live in style and Diego Columbus did just that — for this reason, El Alcázar is the architectural highlight in the colonial district! After arriving one year prior, Diego commissioned the construction of the Alcázar de Colón, the prince's residence, in 1510 under the supervision of several Spanish architects. The construction involved over 1,500 local workers. In the 60 years to follow, this building became the focal point of Spanish rule. Not one nail was used in this building with 22 rooms and 72 doors. What was used was a large amount of sandstone composed of coral. What a visitor will see today, however, is mostly a replica (this is claimed by experts although the government does not like to hear it). The building, the seat of the first Spanish court in the new world, crumbled with time and was first rebuilt in the mid 1950's. Since then, it serves as a museum and can be toured. The Calle las Damas ends at the large plaza in front of the Alcázar de Colón (cafes and galleries can be found on the northern and western sides). This square was a huge construction area in 1990. The goal of this construction was to restore it to its original condition. In doing this it was necessary to use a second square with a small park, fountains and cobblestones.
Very nearby to the Alcázar de Colón was supposedly the first pub in America! Whether Diego Columbus was a regular is not known. Open daily from 9 am to 5 pm (closed Tuesdays); admission: 5 pesos.

Sight in the northern area of the colonial district:

La Ataranzana: This district, characterised by houses from the 15th and 16th centuries, is a popular meeting point for tourists today. It has a number of bars, restaurants and souvenir shops. The focal point of this district is the Reales Atarazanas, the royal naval arsenal. In addition, the first

customs ministry in the new world was also located in this area. The complex can be compared to a similar district in Barcelona.
Hostal Nicolás Nader: The former residential house of Pedro Henríquez Urena, Salomé Urena de Henríquez and President Ulises Heureaux (1845-1899) has now been turned into a hotel.
Ceiba de Colón: At the eastern end of the Atarazana district is the fortress tower, where the remains of a kapok tree can be found nearby. Ceiba de Colón is supposedly the place where Christopher Columbus moored upon arriving at the island on his first voyage.
Santa Bárbara: This church was built in 1562. A distinguishing optical characteristic of the building are the two towers of differing height. Santa Bárbara is located in the quarry which provided most of the building material for Santo Domingo. The bricks for the city wall, built in 1574, also came from this quarry. The freedom fighter Juan Pablo Duarte was baptised in this church.
Other points of interest:
Parque Colón: The park in the middle of Santo Domingo is dedicated to the island's discoverer Christopher Columbus (Spanish: Cristóbal Colón). For this reason, a bronze statue of the seafarer, designed by the French artist E. Gilbert, is on a square in the middle of this park. The park is a common meeting place. Under the old trees, one can sit here in peace and recover from the stress of the big city, if the constant nuisance of the black market peddlers is disregarded. At the northern end of this park are a few small cafes, to the west is the Palacio de Borgellá, to the south, the Santa María la Menor Cathedral and to the west, is the beginning of the pedestrian zone on the Calle El Conde.
Palacio de Borgellá: This palace was built in the second half of the 19th century and is located near Parque Colón. It was formerly the governmental seat for the president and will house the permanent exhibition for the 500-year celebration.
Catedral de Santa María la Menor: Construction began on this, the first cathedral in the new world and one of the most famous buildings in Santo Domingo, between 1514 and 1523. The exact date is not conclusive from the history books. The date of the cathedral's completion is, however, fixed at 1540. The first brick was laid by Diego Colón. However, the phase of construction was ill-fated due to a lack of labourers. Most of the men of this time had the motto: explorer, not construction worker — even the "common man" wanted to follow the great conquerors. The second

attempt at constructing the cathedral was more successful: on March 25, 1521, construction began once more — and was brought to successful completion in 1540. Worth seeing is the late Gothic hall with its beautiful vaulting, the 14 auxiliary chapels with some artistically interesting altars and of course the grave of Christopher Columbus, which was constructed in 1898. Whether the actual bodily remains of the discoverer are really buried here is questioned even by the experts. Seville in Spain still maintains to have the real grave of Columbus: even after 490 years after his death (in 1506) the restless adventurer has still not found his last resting place.

The cathedral is located near the southern part of Parque Colón. Open daily from 9 am to 4 pm.

Callejón: This district was originally intended for the servants of the cathedral. It is located south of the cathedral and some of the old buildings have been restored.

Calle El Conde: This street is the oldest and most important main street and shopping street in Santo Domingo. To the west of Parque Colón, it has been made into a pedestrian zone. The street begins at the Río Ozama and ends at Puerta del Conde, where the ruins of the city wall are found. The "Count's street," was so named after the Count of Penalva, who defended Santo Domingo against the English before the gates of the city in 1655. Calle El Conde has a wide selection of every type of shop (also a well stocked record store — for those who are looking for the newest merengue hits), restaurants (here, too, the trend is toward fast-food) and offers a strong dose of big city atmosphere. The street was only made a pedestrian zone a few years ago. Its modern design is, however, not in accord with the older area of the city nearby.

Monasterio de San Francisco: The ruins of the St. Francis Monastery are located on the corner of Calle Delmonte and Calle Emilio Tejada near the northwestern portion of the colonial district. Built in 1514, this was considered the oldest monastery in the new world. There are two theories for its demise: some think Sir Francis Drake destroyed it during an invasion in 1586. The others think the earthquake of 1673 toppled this building. Either way: today, a stage can be found among the ruins on which cultural events take place.

Casa del Cordón: The absolute superlative: this is the oldest stone building in the new world. It was built by Francisco Garay in 1503. Diego Columbus and his wife lived here before moving into the nearby palace. Why

this house is so named will become apparent to visitors upon seeing it. The facade is decorated with St. Francis knots.
Casa de la Moneda: Located on Calle Arzobispo Meriño is the first mint in the new world. It was built in the middle of the 16th century.
Hospital San Nicolás de Bari: As most of the buildings in the colonial district, this hospital can also boast a superlative: it is both the oldest church and the oldest hospital in the new world. It was built between 1503 and 1508 and housed the chapel of the Holy Virgin of Supreme Grace, the patron saint of the Dominican people. This, however, did not help much over the centuries: only ruins remain of this building.
Fuerte San José: A small fortress and park from which there is a nice view of the harbour. Here, one can escape the hectic atmosphere of the big city for a few moments.
Monumento a Montesinos: Memorial at the entrance to the harbour from Río Ozama located on the southern side of the Malecón.
Malecón: The beach promenade of Santo Domingo is a popular meeting place especially during weekends. Then, the 20 kilometre long portion of beach is transformed into a gigantic outdoor discotheque. One can dine in the small restaurants, drink a cocktail at one of the mobile bars or listen to the different merengue bands. Some of the capital's luxury hotels are located along the Malecón. Guibia Beach is especially popular with surfers.
Sights on the Calle Padre Billini: *Regina Angelorum, Capilla de la Tercer Orden* and the *Dominican Monastery* among others.
Casa de Tostada: The former private home of the poet Francisco de Tostado was built at the beginning of the 16th century. A remarkable aspect: a Gothic window divided in two by a column. This window is said to be the only one of its kind on the American continent. Today, the building houses the "Museum of the Dominican Family." The exhibition includes furniture and articles from the 19th century that present an impression of the everyday (and not so everyday) lifestyle of that time.
Open daily from 9 am to 2:30 pm (closed Wednesdays).

Sights in the western portion of the city centre

Mercado Modelo: A marketplace known for its large selection of handmade crafts particularly. It is located on the Avenida Mella.
Parque Independencia: The park with the Altar de Patria and the Puerta del Conde is well-suited as a starting point when touring the city. Nearby are the ruins of the Fortaleza La Concepción, which was earlier within

the walls of the city and served as the main defence post in the northern portion of Santo Domingo.

Altar de Patria: This "Alter of the homeland," a modern mausoleum, was built in 1976 and is dedicated to the founders of the republic: Duarte, Sánchez and Mella: It is located near the western part of Parque Independencia and is guarded by soldiers. It can only be entered when if wearing appropriate clothing (no shorts or swimming suits; this is also true when visiting churches and monasteries!).

Puerta del Conde: The gate from the 18th century is situated at the western end of Calle El Conde. It is a part of the city's old fortress walls and carries the inscription: "Dulce et decorum est pro patria mori" (It is sweet and beautiful to die for one's country). Beyond the gate is the beginning of Parque Independencia ...

The Zero Kilometre Point: Near Parque Independencia is the depiction of a compass made of bronze which not only shows the 32 directions but also is the zero point for measuring distances to other points on the island. This is also true for the three most important roads in the Dominican Republic: the Carretera Duarte running north, the Carretera Sánchez running south to Haiti as well as the Carretera Las Américas and the Carretera Mella, both running toward the east.

Additional points of interest are:

Botanical Gardens: With around 1.8 million square metres, this is one of the largest in the world. Those who wish, can take a tour on a small train. Especially beautiful: the Japanese area.

Open from 9 am to 5 pm Tuesday to Saturday.

Zoo: The Parque Zoológico is about 10 square kilometres in size and is located in the northern portion of Santo Domingo.

Open 9 am to 5 pm Tuesday to Saturday.

Plaza de la Cultura: This complex was built as a national cultural centre in 1966. In addition to the National Theatre, a number of museums are also found here: Museo del Hombre Dominicano and the Anthropological Museum (open from 10 am to 5 pm Tuesday to Saturday); Museum for History and Geography (daily from 10 am to 5 pm) and the Gallery for Modern Art built in 1976 (daily from 9 am to 5 pm), which has a collection of paintings and sculptures by Dominican artists on display. Concerts, ballets, operas and folklore performances take place in the National Theatre, usually during the weekends. The National Library is also located here. It is open from 8 am to 9 pm on weekdays and from 8 am to noon on Saturdays (closed Sundays).

Santo Domingo / **Practical Information**

Accommodation: Hotel Cervantes, Calle Cervantes 202, Tel: 688-2261, centrally located, 181 rooms, price category 2; Hotel Comodoro, Avenida Bolívar 193, Tel: 687-7141, 87 rooms, price category 2; Hotel Palacio Nicolás de Ovando, Calle Las Damas 53, Tel: 687-3101-04 (historical house, lovingly restored; very nice colonial atmosphere), 45 rooms, price category 3.
Night Life: In the middle of 1990, ''Raffles" (at the corner of Calle Hostos and Calle General Luperón) was one of *the* places to be (live music, pool/billiards and disco).
Population: approximately 2 million.
Shopping: The largest shopping centres are:
- Plaza Central: the newest and most modern shopping centre that Santo Domingo has to offer: located on the corner of Avenida Winston Churchill and Avenida 27 de Febrero.
- Plaza Naco: situated on Avenida Tiradentes at the corner of Calle Fantino Falco.
- National Shopping Center: offering a number of shops and supermarkets on Avenida Abraham Lincoln at the corner of Avenida 27 de Febrero.
- Calle El Conde; the oldest and most traditional shopping street in Santo Domingo; pedestrian zone (see above).
- Avenida Mella: Arts and crafts as far as the eye can see; haggling over the price is part of the enjoyment.
- Avenida Duarte: this is where the Dominicans shop when looking for reasonably priced items. Be cautious: pick-pockets also enjoy ''shopping" here.

Special Events: In the La Atarazana district, a flea market takes place every Sunday; on workdays, there is a nice atmosphere here as well.
Tips: Spending one night in Santo Domingo will usually prove sufficient. One should consider driving into the capital from another city, for instance from Boca Chica. This way one will be spared the stress in ''quieter" surroundings.
Traffic: Not for those with frail nerves — at least within the capital. The first impression is misleading, however: once one is underway, one quickly acquires a feel for the flow of pedestrians, cars and buses. A map is,

however, a definite necessity as street signs are rare. The large Avenidas help in orientation: they all run east-west (more or less) parallel to the coast. The most important arterial Avenidas are John F. Kennedy (leads to the Carretera Duarte, the route to Puerto Plata), 27 de Febrero, Bolívar, Independencia and George Washington (the Malecón). Two bridges span the tributaries of the Río Ozama: the Puente Duarte to the north is in relatively good condition, but is closed to traffic leaving the city in the morning during rush hour. Those coming from Boca Chica must cross this bridge and should then keep left to get to the colonial district (Zona Colonial). The other bridge, "Puente Mella," is open only to traffic leaving the city (bound for Boca Chica).
Travel Agent: Tours within the Dominican Republic, international airline tickets and information are available at Prieto Tours, Avenida Francia 125, Tel: 685-0102 and 688-5715, among others.

Sosúa

"No Problem in Sosúa" — this slogan is printed on T-shirts produced by the thousands in this city. And for those who feel right at home in the touristic bustle, want to take a stroll in the pedestrian zone in the evening and then would like to visit a discotheque later on, this phrase will definitely be true. However, even those seeking peace and quiet, should stay at least one night in Sosúa because Sosúa Beach alone is worth the visit. Sosúa is located about 25 kilometres northeast of Puerto Plata and can be reached by a road in very good condition. The first section of this road leads by the tourist centre Playa Dorado. About three kilometres farther, one has a wonderful view of the landscape: vast sugar cane fields that stretch over rolling hills to the horizon. In the nearby Gran Parada — a few huts and a fork in the road that leads to Santiago de los Caballeros, which is impassible after only a few hundred metres, and therefore, should be avoided — one can make a short stop in Colmado Balbuena to try the region's excellent dairy products. In addition to this, a pastelito with fish might be on the menus. It does, however, have a taste which must definitely be acquired. Continuing on the journey, one will pass Monteliano (with a service station) after a few kilometres, and after that, Puerto Plata's international airport, before arriving in Sosúa.

The city of Sosúa has two different faces. First, one will reach Los Charamicos, a typically Dominican district. Hardly a trace of the tourist boom can be found here. It is more a chaotic Caribbean atmosphere which dominates this area of Sosúa. The streets are astir with people and motorcycles, overflowing fruit stands and restaurants with local flair. Loud music can be heard from the numerous pubs, so loud that one can hardly hear one's own voice. Life pulsates particularly along the Calle Jose E. Kunhard. In blatant contrast to this is the setting in El Batey, located on the other side of Playa Sosúa, which is within the firm grip of the tourists. In the small pedestrian zone, shops and peddlers, restaurants and bars are cramped under the trees. Here, the city conveys a quiet and orderly impression, for which visitors also must pay: the price levels are much higher here than in the neighbouring Los Charamicos district.

Sosúa / **History**

In 1938 at the World Conference for European Refugees, the Dominican Republic resolved to accept Jewish refugees with German or Austrian nationality. From 1940 on, several Jewish families settled in Sosúa as a result. They gradually transformed the landscape into a fertile region. Most were intellectuals, physicians, artists and agriculturally trained specialists. The founding of the cooperative for dairy products followed, and today, the region is known for its excellent dairy and processed meat products. Of this Jewish influence, which is often acclaimed as a tourist attraction, little remains, and visitors must really search for the traces of this influence in Sosúa, with the exception of Jewish names which can still be seen quite frequently.

Sosúa / **Sights**

Calle Pedro Clisante Pedestrian Zone: Particularly during the evening hours, this portion of street closed off to traffic, is the meeting point in Sosúa. Outdoor restaurants, grills and bars (among them, the inevitable oil painting peddlers), but also live music, black market merchants, souvenir shops selling art and kitsch as well as a series of motorcycles on the corner of Calle Duarte: a little of everything can be found here. Some of the bars have a happy hour in the late afternoon (at differing times): drinks are half price — making them at least halfway affordable.

Jewish Synagogue: The synagogue is located near the pedestrian zone and was planned to be remodelled and expanded in the summer of 1990. This unpretentious construction with an adjacent garden actually cannot be considered a point of interest in Sosúa and is hardly worth visiting (except for religious reasons).

Beaches: *Sosúa Beach,* over one kilometre long, is among the nicest beaches that the island has to offer. It extends from the district of Los Charamicos in the east to El Batey in the south and is bordered by two smaller rock formations. On the horizon, one can see Puerto Plata and Pico Isabela de Torres. The times, however, when the atmosphere of the beach was tranquil, have since past. Meanwhile, dozens of restaurants and souvenir shops housed in provisional stands have settled along the beach. The local residents, however, do not let this disturb their game of dominoes.

A fair ground atmosphere dominates the coastline — and the bay, where all sorts of water sports are offered. Surfboards and sail boats can be rented here. The real "hit," however, are the small but powerful motorboats: these are certainly not cheap and anything but quiet.

For those who would like to experience the bay in a more peaceful setting: there are tours in glass-bottom boats available (El Hippocampo, 50 pesos, about one-half hour). From the boat, one can observe the underwater flora and fauna in the bay through the turquoise-coloured water. The tour itself is better than the sign advertising it: "Unmistakable. Famous for its versatility. The only boat where you can clearly view the plants and aquatic animals and coral in the bay of Sosúa."

Additional beaches are the approximately 300-metre long bay *Sand Castle Beach,* on which the luxurious Sand Castle Beach Hotel is located, about 10 kilometres west of Sosúa and the small *La Playita* north of the El Batey district. Situated here are the luxury hotels Casa Marina, Sosúa-by-the-Sea, Sosúa Paradise and Paradise Larimar.

Sosúa / **Practical Information**

Accommodation: Elena's, Tel: 571-2872, 20 rooms, located outside the city on a mountain slope overlooking Sosúa, take the road to the right of the Texaco station on the outskirts of the city up the slope, new hotel, run by the Americans Elaine and Frank, very friendly atmosphere, beautiful view all the way to Puerto Plata during the evening, swimming pool, the fairly long trip to Elena's is worth it, price category 2, includes breakfast; Auberge du Canada, Calle Julio Arceno, Tel: 571-3025, is in the louder district of La Charamicos, but is quiet despite this, very near to Playa Sosúa, Monica from Quebec runs this hotel and speaks French, English and Spanish, price category 2; Sosúa Ocean Front Guest-House, El Batey district, Tel: 571-2284, 7 rooms in small bungalows equipped with a kitchenette, nice view of the bay all the way to Puerto Plata, near the pedestrian zone, run by Félix G. Koch, a Jewish man who has lived a number of years in Sosúa, price category 2.

Banks: Banco Popular, Calle Los Llibre 1, north of the intersection with Carretera Sosúa (open 8:30 am to 5:30 pm); Banco Regional, Calle Alejo Martínez (open 8:30 am to 1 pm and 2 to 4:30 pm). In addition, the Banco de Reservas has mobile currency stands which are usually located near the taxi stand near the Sosúa Park. At these stands, the exchange rate is often somewhat better, but one must also wait longer.

Cock-Fights: These take place in Club Gallístico Sosúa, Los Charamicos at the following times: Tuesdays from 10 am, Wednesdays from 4 pm and Saturdays and Sundays from 10 am. The matches end between 6 and 10 pm depending on the number of individual fights.

Information: The tourist newspaper ''The Puerto Plata News" usually has a special section on Sosúa in most issues. Here, one will find information, tips and special events. The ''News" is available free of charge in hotels and restaurants, or by contacting the editorial office: Sosúa Business Services, Calle Pedro Clisante 12, Tel: 571-3451.

Language Courses: Learn Spanish on holidays, why not? Those who plan on staying for a longer time on the island will find the effort worthwhile. The best tip in Sosúa: Franklin Guzman Arias, Sosúa Business Services, Calle Pedro Clisante (in the city centre), Tel: 571-3452 and 571-3451. Courses are in English and Spanish. Class size is 6 participants. Prices: a three-month course costs around 300 pesos. Shorter intensive training is available on request.

Night Life: The Scherezade Disco (Tel: 571-2430) is located in the Sand Castle Beach Resort about 10 kilometres outside of Sosúa toward Puerto Plata and is one of the hottest tips for an entertaining evening (good music including merengue with music videos).

Offices: For those looking for office space in Sosúa, whether they want a mailing address, telefax service, use of a copier, a contact address in case of an emergency, or other office service, then Sosúa Business Services it the place to contact (Calle Pedro Clisante 12, Tel: 571-3451 or 571-3452, Fax: 571-3453). Sosúa Business Services is located above the Casablanca Bar).

Pharmacy: Farmacia San Rafael, Carretera Sosúa (on the main street toward Cabarete, near the Texaco station), Tel: 571-2515.

Physicians: Medical assistance, house calls and 24 hour emergency service: Centro Médico Sosúa, Calle Alejo Martínez, Tel 571-2305 and 571-3949 (near the One Ocean Place Hotel) and Grupo Médico Sosúa, on the main street in Los Charamicos (the older district in Sosúa), Tel: 571-2528.

In addition, there are two private clinics run by Dr. Garcia (with a dental practice) and Dr. Nelson.

Police: Tel: 571-2233.

Post Office: The post office is located in the older district of Sosúa on the main street of Los Charamicos (open from 8 am to noon and 2:30 to 5 pm).

Shopping: The Calle Pedro Clisante is the centre for (not only) shopping. The most shops and boutiques are located here.

Supermarket: Groceries and beverages can be purchased from the satisfactory selection in Sosúa Supermarket, Carretera Sosúa, diagonally across from the Texaco station.

Transportation: Caribe Tours offers daily connections from Sosúa to Santo Domingo (travel time: 5 hours). It takes half an hour to reach Cabarete (price is around three pesos, the best point of departure is Hotel Las Almendros, price for the continuing trip to Río San Juan is about eight pesos). By Guagua, the trip to Puerto Plata costs about four pesos; the best departure point is the Texaco station on the Carretera Sosúa. The best place to get Motoconchos is at the west end of the Calle Pedro Clisante and for a trip within the city limits one will pay two to a maximum of three pesos. Be careful: a common souvenir of Sosúa is the so-called "Sosúa birthmark," these are burn marks that the passenger can get from the motorcycle's exhaust pipe.

Those travelling by taxi will have to dig deeper into their pockets. Prices are usually negotiated. This should be considered a part of the deal by passengers. Taxi drivers will first try to set the price as high as possible. Afterwards, they will become "generous" and still strike a good deal for themselves in the process. For common destinations, the following prices may be used as guidelines (prices given for single/return trip): Puerto Plata

80/150 pesos, Cabarete 50/100 pesos and the international airport 50/100 pesos. Those requiring further information should contact Tel: 571-2797 or 571-3097. These prices are only intended as guidelines. The price paid usually depends on one's ability to bargain. Private ''taxis" are less expensive, but if there is an accident, one must expect insurance problems. As a general rule: the price should be agreed upon in advance.
Travel Agency: Information about Sosúa and tours available in the surrounding regions is available in the El Batey district: Costa Tour, Calle Alejo Martinez 9, Tel: 571-2112 and 571-2169.

Souvenirs

For many travellers, the search for the appropriate souvenir begins shortly after arrival in the Dominican Republic. This might not be a bad idea: if one waits until the last minute in the hopes of finding the right souvenir at the airport, then one will usually be penalised with prices that are almost twice as high as normal.
The most popular souvenirs from the Dominican Republic are:
Cigars: These are most reasonably priced when purchased in the regions producing tobacco near Santiago. The best opportunity to purchase cigars is at the end of a tour of a cigar factory.
Rum: can be found everywhere in the country on every street corner. The prices are far less expensive than in other countries. One must however, check the customs regulations in one's home country to be sure one does not exceed the duty-free allowance.
Amber: is frequently available in the souvenir shops on the northern coast, especially in Puerto Plata and Sosúa.
Larimar: is available almost everywhere.
Oil Paintings: On the streets and beaches, there are often merchants with their ''portable galleries." The artistic standards of these paintings is, however, usually quite low: the Dominican paintings in these collections are usually copied from naive style of Haitian colleagues, who are better known, and above all, better artists. The merchants sell anything that is colourful. The most common motifs are landscapes and sunsets. Also a typical motive: masses of people (usually only heads) spread over the entire picture.

Other Souvenirs: In addition to these souvenirs, weavings made from coconut palms are also available (especially along the road from Puerto Plata to Santiago) as well as mahogany masks and statues. (Note: selling the valuable tropical wood is common practice in the Dominican Republic, as it is in other tropical countries. Every tourist can do his part in saving these forests by not purchasing products made from mahogany). Other carvings made from talc or other woods can also make an appropriate souvenir.

It is generally true that even domestic products are much more expensive in the duty-free shops at the airports than in the country itself. The selection in the duty-free shop in Santo Domingo is extensive. The prices for international products like perfumes, cigarettes and alcoholic beverages are, however, quite high. It is better to take advantage of the duty-free selection available on the flight home.

→*Amber, Larimar, Rum, Tobacco*

Suggested Travel Routes

In addition to the beauty of the landscapes and nature, the lack of transportation and the poor road conditions make the following routes for travel through the Dominican Republic more sensible and practicable:

Route 1: Santo Domingo — Boca Chica — San Pedro de Macoris — La Romana — Higüey — Bavaro/east coast

Route 2: Santo Domingo — Azua — Barahona — Lago Enriquillo

Route 3: Santo Domingo — Bonao — Jarabacoa — La Vega — Santiago — Puerto Plata

Route 4: Puerto Plata — Sosúa — Cabarete — Río San Juan — Nagua — Sánchez — Las Terrenas — Samaná

Route 5: Puerto Plata — Luperón — Laguna Salada — Monte Cristi

Taxes at Entry

As of May 1, 1990, tourists must buy a so-called tourist card for $10, which is a type of entry tax when arriving in the Dominican Republic. This card must be purchased directly after arrival, and this usually means long waits at the counter (usually, only one is open). Citizens of the United Kingdom are exempt from this tax. Upon leaving the Dominican Republic, a tax

of $10 is also charged. The regulations concerning this tax are, however, unclear. For those travelling by package tour: the exit taxes have usually already been paid by the tour organisation upon delivery of the ticket.
→*Mandatory Currency Exchange*

Telephones

One can by no means count on the option of using public telephones in telephone booths, in public buildings, bars and restaurants: they are frequently out of order or the telephone lines are hopelessly overburdened. If they should happen to function despite this, then calls can only be made locally.
One good and convenient alternative is offered by the telecommunications company CODETEL. This company operates around 80 telecommunications centres in the entire country, which can be found in all of the larger cities (usually housed in containers).
The most important centres can be found in:
Santo Domingo: Aeropuerto International de Las Américas, Avenida Bolívar 1004, Avenida 30 de Marzo 12, Avenida 27 de Febrero 247, Hermanas Mirabal, Avenida Independencia Km 6 and at Calle Duarte 14;
Puerto Plata: Calle Beller 58 and Aeropuerto International de Puerto Plata;
Cabarete: Carretera Sosúa — Cabarete;
Sosúa: Calle Dr. Ross, corner of Calle Alejo Martinez;
Barahona: Calle Uruguay, corner of Calle General Cabral;
San Cristóbal: Calle Palo Hincado 14;
Bonao: Calle 27 de Febrero 69;
La Vega: Calle J. Rodriguez, corner of Calle Duvergé;
Santiago: Avenida Circunvalación 21 and Avenida Estrella Sadhalá;
Moca: Calle Nuestra Señora del Rosario and Calle 16 de Julio;
Samaná: Calle San Bárbara 2 Oeste;
San Francisco de Macoris: Avenida 27 de Febrero 54;
Sánchez: Calle Duarte 4;
Boca Chica: Calle Duarte, corner of Avenida Carrocal;
Higüey: Calle Bertilio Alfau 160;
Juan Dolio: Plaza Quisqueya;
La Romana: Calle Duarte 128 and Calle Padre Abreu 1 (Unicentro);
San Pedro de Macoris: Avenida Independencia 111 and 127.

Tobacco

Finally something which was already on the island before Christopher Columbus arrived: tobacco was cultivated on the island well before the ''discovery" and was highly valued because of its (astonishing but true) favourable medicinal side effects.
Today, tobacco is one of the most important export goods in the Dominican Republic and the excellent quality of Dominican products is highly valued. Experts even dare compare Dominican tobacco and cigars to Cuban products.
The focal point of the tobacco industry is Santiago. Here, there are numerous cigar factories, which also offer tours. Some are located directly on the Calle Duarte north of Santiago. If ones turns off of the main street and drives into the town of Villa Gonzáles, then one can visit the production area of the Procapar firm (in Palmarejo, Villa González, Tel: 583-5084 and 583-5185). There are 70 workers, each producing 500 cigars per eight-hour workday. One can watch all stages of production from the drying process to the hand rolling and finishing of the cigars. Only Santiago tobacco is used in this process — with the exception of the leaf used in rolling the cigars, which is imported from Nicaragua due to the high demands on quality.
One advantage: tourists seldom come here, the employees are very friendly and helpful to visitors. A small disadvantage: explanations for future ''specialists" are only in Spanish. But as a compensation, visitors have the opportunity to purchase cigars at a very reasonable price.
Tip: it is best to buy directly from the factory — one will not find a better price anywhere else.

Tourist Information

The tourist boom has only reached the Dominican Republic in recent years. This is evident in terms of tourist information. The few Tourist Information Offices (in Santo Domingo, Puerto Plata and Sosúa among other cities) usually have very little printed material. This material is often not up-to-date and inaccurate. The same is also true for the Ministry of Tourism on the Malecón in Santo Domingo (Secretaría de Estado de Tourismo, Avenida George Washington): one can forego the trip here — the information one receives here is not worth mentioning. There are also infor-

mation offices at Las Américas International Airport, La Unión Airport near Puerto Plata, in Puerto Plata (Malecón 20, Tel: 586-3676), in Santiago (Ayuntamiento, Tel: 582-5885), Jimaní, Samaná and Boca Chica.
Those looking for information on the island should best take the private route. Many travel agencies and travel organisations are usually very willing to provide information on the region, even though no trip is booked. One will always acquire the most information through personal contact since the Dominicans are justifiably very proud of their country.
Tourist Information in other countries:
United States: 485 Madison Avenue, 2nd Floor, New York, New York, 10022, Tel: (212)-826-0750 or 800-752-1151 (toll-free).
Canada: 24 Bellair Street, Toronto, Ontario, M5R 2C7, Tel: (416)-928-9188; 1464 Crescent Street, Montréal, Québec, H3A 2B6, Tel: (514)843-3418.

Transportation in the Dominican Republic

Transportation in the Dominican Republic / **By Car**

When planning travel within the Dominican Republic overall, or when planning daily routes, one should take the road conditions into consideration — they are often very poor. Many roads are often covered with potholes and are little more than a sand path; even to cover short distances, it can take up to hours. Quite often the maximum speed that can be driven on Dominican roads is 30 km/h. This is, however not true for the roads between the larger cities like Santo Domingo, La Romana, Santiago, Puerto Plata and Barahona. These are the only paved roads that are in good condition throughout. The most **important roadways in the Dominican Republic are:**
- the *Carretera Duarte* from Santo Domingo heading north to Santiago and which then runs through the Cibao Valley. It then takes a slight detour to Puerto Plata (near José E. Bisonó) before continuing northeast via Esperanza, Laguna Salada and Villa Vásquez and ending in Monte Cristi. The first 30 kilometres has two lanes. A toll of 50 centavos is charged for this portion (it is best to have exact change). When driving toward the capital, no toll is charged;
- the *Carretera Sánchez,* which runs from Santo Domingo west via San Cristóbal, Baní and Azua to Barahona ending up in the region bordering Haiti. The last few kilometres of this asphalt road, however already show

signs of wear. Tourists who are driving to Lago Enriquillo will have to use this road;

- the *Carretera Las Américas* extends from Santo Domingo eastwards. Shortly after leaving the city limits of Santo Domingo, the street lives up to its name: at short intervals, cement pillars appear with the coats of arms and names of all of the countries in Middle and South America along the road (given that the pillars have not since been removed). Be cautious: one should not be distracted by this geographic tutorial. Speed is often checked by radar along this portion of motorway. It is, however, more common to be stopped by the police, who are positioned at almost the same intervals as the pillars, for no reason whatsoever.

Shortly before reaching the international airport, there is a toll booth (50 centavos). This first stretch of the Carretera Las Américas can certainly be considered one of the most beautiful airport roads in the world: the road leads alongside the turquoise ocean under rows of palm trees. A short break at one of the numerous rest stops is worthwhile, not only if one would like to, like many Dominicans, catch a quick dinner by fishing in the churning ocean. Beyond the airport, the road leads past Boca Chica toward Juan Dolio, San Pedro de Macoris and continues on to La Romana and Altos de Chavón. The main road ends at this point. The roads continuing to Higüey and the eastern coast are not in as good condition, and covering the kilometres to follow requires much more time than do the last few kilometres to La Romana.

Visitors who wish to drive in the Dominican Republic can use their own national **driving licence.** The international driving licence is recognized here as well. **Speed limits** in the Dominican Republic: 80 km/h on the sections of the roads with more than one lane (similar to motorways) and 40 km/h within city limits. However, after driving only a few kilometres, it will become apparent that these "regulations" are considered only "recommendations" by most of the Dominicans. Otherwise: the Dominicans drive as fast as the conditions allow.

Transportation in the Dominican Republic / **Public Transportation**

Public transportation in the Dominican Republic is dominated by private companies. In addition to this, the following can also be said about the public transportation available in the Dominican Republic:

Buses: All of the larger cities and towns are serviced by bus companies serving the entire country. They offer different classes of travel: from the simple cross-country bus to the air conditioned luxury bus equipped with a bar and stewardess. The most significant bus companies are *Caribe Tours* and *Metro Servicios;* in addition to these, *Terra Bus* and *Companía Nacional* offer transportation by bus.

Taxis: Taxis are available near all of the larger hotels, on public squares or by ordering one by telephone (this is, however, a complicated process in most cases). ''Publicos" appears on the side of the taxis. Important: As taximeters are all but unknown, one should ask the price in advance. One must definitely negotiate the price before the trip, to avoid unpleasant surprises upon arrival at one's destination. Frequently, private cars are also used to offer taxi services. These are, however, not marked as ''Publicos."

Motoconchos: Motoconchos are certainly the most commonly used means of transportation in the country. These privately owned motorcycles (usually 50 cc) will take anyone along, they stop everywhere and can get to the most remote areas using the worst roads. They are, however, used mainly for shorter trips within the towns. A price should definitely be negotiated before departure. Depending on the length of the trip, prices range from one to three pesos. Those who do not agree upon a price in advance can end up with an unpleasant — and expensive — surprise. Tourists (''gringos") are popular victims of the Motoconcho drivers.

Guaguas: How many passengers will fit into a Japanese van? In the Dominican Republic, this question seems to be answered daily with a new record. The ''Guaguas," vans, are ubiquitous in the country. One will see them in every city and town on the public squares. These are usually operated by private entrepreneurs and run (more or less) regularly according to a defined schedule serving specified routes. What remains unspecified is the number of passengers each transports. Guaguas will become quickly conspicuous to visitors, because one could estimate that one-third of the passengers are on or attached to, rather than in the vehicle. 25-30 passengers in one van are not rare. In addition to the closed buses (poor air), open pick-up trucks are also frequently used (during longer trips, a hat or scarf is advantageous).

Prices are relatively reasonable. An average price is impossible to quote because charges usually depend on the road conditions — and it is not uncommon that ''gringos" are charged more than local residents. Here

too, one should by all means agree upon a price in advance. It is also helpful to pay in exact change at the end of the trip. This will hinder the possibility of further negotiations.
Those who would like to experience a portion of the Dominican lifestyle up-close, should take a ride in a Guagua at least once: An adventure in the most restricted space, wedged between people and animals, with breathing difficulties and feet that have fallen asleep — this, of course, when sitting inside; when outside the vehicle, or if one only found space while hanging halfway out the door, one experiences fits of panic and eyes squeezed shut from sheer terror, piously promising oneself to *never* again set foot into such a van — until the next time: a ride in a Guagua is almost inevitable in the Dominican Republic.
Expreso: The luxury version of a Guaguas: somewhat ''fewer" passengers, fewer stops, but slightly more expensive because of this.
Airplanes: There are a number of private airlines which serve cities like Santiago Domingo, Puerto Plata, Santiago, Las Terrenas, (El Portillo), Samaná and La Romana.
Information in regard to departure times and prices is available through: Victoria Air, Aerotaxis Portillo S.A., Servicio Aéreo Dominicano, and Aeronaves Dominicanas among others. All are located in the Aeropuerto de Herrera, Santo Domingo.
→*Car Rental, Police, Buses*

Travel Literature

Even in the larger cities, there are very few bookstores. The booksellers as well as the authors primarily blame distribution problems for the insufficient shipments. As is the case with printed tourist information: it is best to get travel literature in your home country. This is true for books printed in English as well as other European languages. Those who speak Spanish will have a less difficult time. Political literature is quite readily available.
What can be highly recommended for those interested in the national parks is the book by Jürgen Hoppe ''The National Parks of the Dominican Republic (in English and Spanish). The most significant national parks on the island are presented in this book including their most important flora and fauna.

Travelling to the Dominican Republic

Which is the best port of entry to the Dominican Republic — Puerto Plata or Santo Domingo? Both airports regularly serve international air traffic especially from the USA and Canada. Direct flights are offered by a number of airlines. Those confronted with the question which of these two airports is the "better" should choose **Puerto Plata.** Advantages: the city is smaller and less hectic. Those travelling on their own will find a hotel room more easily — the first few hours after an overseas flight are nerve-wracking. In addition, the neighbouring town of Sosúa offers another accommodation alternative in which one can find a hotel relatively quickly. Furthermore, most of the nicest and most interesting sections of beach are found on the northern coast.

In contrast **Santo Domingo** has the hectic atmosphere of a big city. This can be exhausting, especially for visitors who have just arrived. If one does not pay attention or is not familiar with the mentality and price structures of the island, in most cases one will quickly pay (literally) for an "introductory course." The southern coast, on which Santo Domingo is located, is far more developed and more heavily populated than the quieter northern coast, however, its landscapes are less attractive.

Travelling to the Dominican Republic / **By Air**

Charter flights will most often prove to be the least expensive option. The travel time from Europe is about 11 hours. During the off season, air fares can be as much as 30% cheaper. Upon landing at the international airport in Santo Domingo, it usually takes quite a while until luggage can be claimed. This time is best used to exchange money into the local currency (pesos) in the arrivals hall. The arrivals hall is located before customs (the exchange rate here is the official exchange rate valid all over the Dominican Republic). Here one has the time and the opportunity to do so, which is not always the case after leaving the airport. It might also happen that one finds himself in need of cash shortly after arrival. One must definitely be cautious in the airport: upon arrival at the Las Américas International Airport in Santo Domingo, one should never let one's luggage out one one's sight and above all never let go of it. Shortly after customs there is a horde of porters who will try to grab the bags from the newcomers. Those who let themselves be outwitted will have to pay

dearly: for the few steps to the parking area, the taxi or the buses, a price of $15 is demanded!
During the middle of 1990, a new airport terminal (an expansion to the old building) was opened. This was supposed to relieve the congestion in the completely obsolete terminal by adding to the capacity by 500,000 passengers per year. What effect this has had on the problem with the porters remains in question. Newcomers should still be cautious. Those who would rather wait for official intervention through the police will wait in vain: the police are the porters' friends and guardians...

Travelling to the Dominican Republic / **Practical Information**

Passengers arriving at the international airport in Santo Domingo at a late hour should best look for accommodation nearby. On the opposite side of the Las Américas Highway (about 500 metres from the airport) is a simple but clean hotel in the price category 1, which is well-suited for the first night after arrival or the night before an early departure. Another option is to look for a hotel in Boca Chica, about 10 kilometres away.

Travelling to the Dominican Republic / **By Ship**

The island of Hispaniola is a popular port of call for cruises, especially with American and Canadian cruises in the Caribbean. The starting point for such cruises is usually Miami. The cruises are usually quite expensive and offer only a limited amount of time to spend in the Dominican Republic. The ports in which the cruise ships most often stop are the Samaná region with the island of Cayo Levantado, Puerto Plata, Casa de Campo and Santo Domingo.

Travelling to the Dominican Republic / **Package Tours**

In recent years, the Dominican Republic has increased drastically in popularity among package tour destinations. This boom has not only brought positive developments to the Caribbean Island. Above all, the Dominican officials no longer are willing to accept that about 90% of foreign currencies spent by tourists in the Dominican Republic end up flowing back out. It is usually the hotel chains, the airlines, package tour organisations and automobile rental agencies that provide for this re-transfer of funds.

Despite this: those looking forward to a relaxing and lazy holiday will find that the package tour organisations offer the best alternative. These organisations also offer a more or less broad selection of optional tours and programmes, which provides the opportunity to become better acquainted with the country and its people.
Those who are not scared off by a certain degree of stress, and who do not want to spend every day on the same beach, are better off travelling on their own. An optimal holiday form is certainly a combination: first relaxation in a beach hotel, that is almost always least expensive when booked in the form of a package tour, and then exploring the island on one's own, using the bus or a rental car.
→*Boca Chica, Entry Taxes, Mandatory Currency Exchange*

Vaccinations

No vaccinations are required for entering the Dominican Republic. However, a malaria prophylactic is recommended for those who plan to travel to Haiti or the regions in the interior of the Dominican Republic near the Haitian border. In addition, everyone travelling to the Dominican Republic should check the length of time that has elapsed since their last vaccinations for tetanus and polio. If necessary, these vaccinations should be refreshed.

Visas

A visa is usually not required when staying only up to 90 days. One does however need a valid passport. Upon arrival one must buy a so-called "tourist card" *(→Entry Taxes)*. The price for this is $10 and cannot be paid in pesos. Therefore, one should definitely carry dollars in the form of cash, otherwise one must first wait to exchange money — not the optimal way to begin a holiday. If travelling on a package tour, the agency may have already taken care of this — be sure to ask so that the fee is not paid twice. Citizens of some countries are exempt from the entry tax. Although, in some cases, entry into the Dominican Republic is possible with only proper identification, which is often praised by the government officials, one should definitely bring along a passport.

Information about entry to the Dominican Republic and problems with visas is available through the Immigration Office, Department of Foreign Affairs, Santo Domingo, Tel: 682-2535 and 685-2505.

Whales

According to the International Whale Commission (IWC) in the Netherlands the number of whales is steadily decreasing worldwide: In the southern polar region, there are only 500 blue whales left — at 30 metres in length, the largest creatures on earth. Furthermore, there are 2,000 finback whales, 1,500 right whales, 800 dwarf finback whales — and about 4,000 humpback whales. About 3,000 of these humpback whales still live in the Atlantic. Between November and April, only one goal is apparent to 80% of them: they are drawn to the waters off the coast of the Dominican Republic and especially the outer regions of the Bahía de Samaná to mate. At this time, tours are offered departing from Samaná to observe the whales in the open seas: aboard the boats, the efforts of several male whales to win the affection of a female can be observed with relatively little danger. Whales are warm-blooded mammals, giving birth to living offspring. Whales also need air to breathe, and therefore, must surface occasionally. They can then be recognized by the spouting water. This makes them relatively easy to locate for observers. The mating ritual includes the whales colliding above the surface of the water.

The whales usually do not attack the observation boats. Most of the organisations offering these tours as well as their boat captains usually have years of experience with these types of observation tours. However, one should not get too close to the courting whales: in their overwhelming passion, they could very well overlook a boat...

Whales are loners. During the remaining months of the year, they live dispersed in the North American waters around Maine, Iceland or Greenland. After mating, the animals go their own ways. A year later, the female returns to the Bahía de Samaná to give birth to her offspring. In the following year, she is ready once more to take part in the mating ritual — and the competition among the male whales begins anew...

One phenomenon which is still not fully explained occupies numerous scientists who position their boats every year off the coast of Samaná: the whales communicate through various forms of singing. However, only the male whales ''sing.'' Although they spend most of the year alone, upon returning to Samaná, they quite obviously recognize each other by means of their ''songs.'' Each year there appears to be a ''hit'' which is then used by most of the whales as a form of common communication.

Whales / **Practical Information**

Whale observation tours are offered, departing from Samaná and Sánchez (some in luxurious excursion boats). Those who would like to experience this natural spectacle in a more ''modest'' atmosphere must expect to pay a price of about 800 pesos per boat for the tour lasting approximately three hours. Information is available at (among other places): Whales Samaná, Samaná/Malecón. In Puerto Plata, Amigo Tours offers charter flights from Puerto Plata and Playa Dorada to the airport in Samaná with transfer to the bay (day-trip).
→*Samaná, Sánchez*

Wildlife and Animals

Characteristic of the fauna in the Dominican Republic are the large proportions of lower animals and the diversity of birds. On the other hand, there are relatively few mammals. Worth mentioning are: the mountain iguana, two species of Jutías (West Indian rodents), the American crocodile, the national bird, the Cigua Palmera and different species of parrots as well as sea cows and hump-backed whales.
Information about the country's fauna is available at the Museum of Natural History, in the Cultural Centre in Santo Domingo (Tel: 689-0106) or at the National Parks Director's Office (Dirección Nacional de Parques, Calle las Damas 6, Tel: 685-1315). About 15% of the island has been declared a national park or similar natural reserve. The best known and most important regions are the national parks Los Haitíses, Isla Cabritos, Jaragua, Armando Bermúdez and Del Este. Usually, one needs permission to go into these areas. For the most part, however, boat tours and day-trips into this region are offered without the organiser having been granted permission. The participants on these tours need not worry about these formalities. However, those travelling into these regions on their own (for example, climbing the Pico Duarte in the Armando Bermúdez National Park), must apply for the necessary permit at the National Park Administration.

Women Travelling Alone

Foreign women are still considered an ''attraction," especially in the beach resorts which are not heavily frequented by tourists. One will be ''marvelled at" and most certainly approached, but hardly ever harassed (excepting the wandering hairdressers on the beach offering their braiding services). However, one should also make one's own contribution and forego topless bathing.

The Dominican Republic is nowhere near being an ''island of love," but the ''business" of short-term affairs is flourishing. The Dominicans who tell of their girlfriends in London, Berlin and New York are not few in numbers. Those looking for a small adventure will have no difficulties finding one here. One should, however, not forget that changing partners frequently is common. Strongholds of this phenomenon are particularly the beach in Puerto Plata, Sosúa and on the southern coast near Juan Dolio. Be cautious: AIDS is also present in the Dominican Republic, which is especially directed toward male tourists, but is also an increasingly important warning for female visitors as well.

In general: in case love at first sight is something else at second sight, but the marriage was already a few days ago, then the Ministry of Tourism has a brochure with the appropriate tips especially for this ''emergency" entitled *Quick Divorces:* ''You will hopefully never need to take advantage of this service, but if you need to dissolve the marital ties to your partner promptly, then you can do this here without losing any time. According to Dominican law, a marriage involving a foreign citizen can be annulled within 24 hours if one of the partners can produce a notarised document in which the divorce is mutually agreed upon and a Dominican attorney brings the case before court. There are law practices specialising in these cases." There are, however, also at least a dozen offices that have specialised in international/Dominican marriages.